Sweet Home
Alabama

Chip Cooper

Shuttle – Main Engines

The most visible symbol of Huntsville's role in bringing America into the space age, the U. S. Space and Rocket Center is the home of the Earth's largest space museum and the U. S. Space Camp. Eminent rocket scientist Dr. Wernher von Braun spearheaded America's rush to the moon and selected Huntsville's Redstone Arsenal as its research center– dramatically altering Huntsville's destiny forever.

Sweet Home Alabama

Food for Family and Friends
from the
Heart of the South

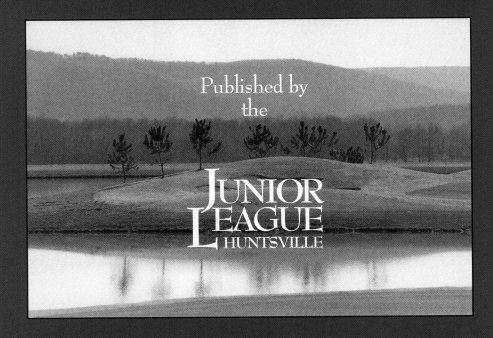

Published by
the

JUNIOR
LEAGUE
HUNTSVILLE

Sweet Home Alabama

The Junior League of Huntsville is an organization of women committed to promoting voluntarism and to improving the community through the effective action and leadership of trained volunteers. Its purpose is exclusively educational and charitable.

The Junior League of Huntsville reaches out to women of all races, religions, and national origins who demonstrate an interest in and a commitment to voluntarism and to the community.

Published by
Junior League of Huntsville
Cookbook Publications
P.O. Box 816
Huntsville, Alabama 35804
(205) 883-9120
Copyright© 1995 Junior League of Huntsville

First Printing: 1995   20,000 copies

Food Photographer   Bill Sweikart

Location Photographer   Chip Cooper

Chef and Food Stylist   Christian Sowder
assisted by   Lynda Claydon Sowder

Manufactured in the United States of America by
Favorite Recipes® Press
2451 Atrium Way, Nashville, Tennessee 37230

ISBN: 0-9618113-1-5
Library of Congress No. 95-60309

Front Cover was underwritten by Aline Blair Lary, President 1954–1955
Back Cover was underwritten by Betsy Jones Lowe, President 1973–1974

Covered Bridge with Winter Sky

Chip Cooper

The Madison County Nature Trail on beautiful Green Mountain is
an area for nature study and wildlife conservation as well as
a tranquil and picturesque retreat. The covered bridge on the
nature trail is a replica of the covered bridges of the 19th century.

Photograph right:
Grilled Salmon with
Avocado Citrus Salsa

Cover:
Pears Poached in Red Wine

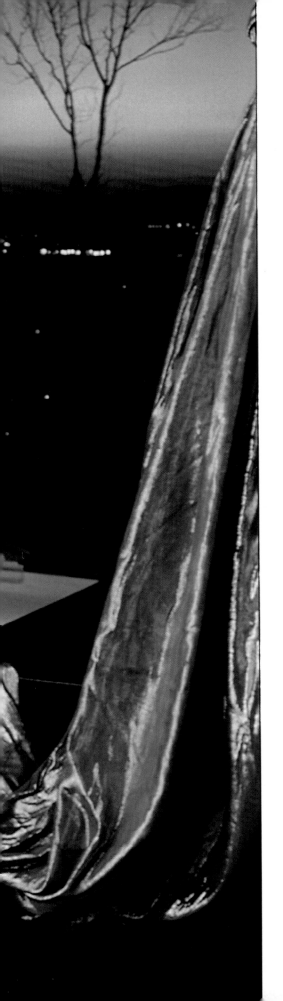

Table of Contents

❧

Introduction

Today we see a resurgence of interest in home life — a yearning to return to home and hearth. In spite of our fast-paced lives, we seek to recapture the days when life was simpler and families and friends had more time together. Food and the entire ritual of meals prepared at home are often entwined in those fond memories. Americans are returning to entertaining at home; Alabamians never stopped.

Southerners have a rich history of cooking and entertaining at home with confident grace and easy style. From the simplest impromptu gatherings to the most elaborately celebrated holidays, opening our homes to family and friends lies at the heart of Southern hospitality.

Alabamians take advantage of our temperate climate and naturally beautiful surroundings whether enjoying a casual lakeside picnic or an elegant dinner under the stars. Even inside our homes, nature's bounty is enjoyed year round. Fresh herbs and vegetables supply our tables, and we are forever combing our gardens for the greenery and flowers that bring charm to even the simplest gatherings. The way we cook complements this easy lifestyle.

Many selections in **Sweet Home Alabama** feature innovative ways to use the fresh ingredients that have always been integral to Southern cooking. Grilled recipes, quick casual recipes, and selections to please a crowd suit our busy lives. We've also included some honored favorites that deserve revisiting. In case you've forgotten the irresistible taste and aroma of homemade rolls, a cake brimming with fresh peaches, or tempting soufflés, we offer our versions of these classics. Only the goodness is old-fashioned.

Within these pages, our distinctive heritage takes center stage in compelling black and white photographs of the region and color photographs of fabulous food in evocative settings. Excerpts from the writings of Alabama authors recall the simple joys of home.

"Sweet Home Alabama" isn't just a clever phrase. It represents the affection with which Alabamians regard the place we call home. Wherever you make your home, we hope you will find that these offerings enhance your time spent with family and friends.

Split Rail Fence and Log Cabin

Chip Cooper

The pioneers of the 19th century come to life on the grounds of the Burritt Museum and Park. Originally the estate of Dr. William Henry Burritt, the museum site on Round Top Mountain now includes the mansion and a historic park of relocated pioneer structures. This imposing house, now a museum of local history, is adjacent to majestic Monte Sano Mountain and commands a spectacular view of Huntsville and beyond.

This photograph was underwritten by Kakki Jordan Brooks, President 1988–1989; Ellen Earls Robinson, President 1986–1987

Photograph right:
Huntsville Botanical Gardens.
Southern Vegetable Terrine

Overleaf:
Artichokes with Basil Béarnaise

Appetizers & Beverages

❦

*That's what we said
on the softness of that
expansive Alabama night
a long long time ago
when you invited me to dine
and I had never dined before
but had always just
"had supper."*

—Zelda Fitzgerald
The Collected Writings

This photograph was underwritten by Martha Holliman Simms Rambo, President 1950–1951;
Cynthia Bagby Richardson, President 1993–1994

Cheese Tarts with Apples

An outstanding appetizer—fresh, pretty and elegant. Be sure to use only tart apples.

Combine 16 ounces of the cream cheese and the sour cream in a bowl; mix well. In another bowl, blend the remaining 8 ounces of cream cheese, Camembert cheese, bleu cheese and Gruyère cheese.

Line two 8-inch springform pans or pretty molds with cheesecloth. Spread the sour cream mixture over the bottom of each springform pan or mold. Layer the pecans and cheese mixture over the top.

Chill, covered, for 2 days or for up to 3 weeks.

Serve on decorative plates with sliced apples.

May freeze, wrapped in foil, for up to 6 months. Add the apples after defrosting.

24 ounces cream cheese, softened
2 tablespoons sour cream
4 ounces Camembert cheese
4 ounces bleu cheese
4 ounces Gruyère cheese
5 ounces pecans, chopped
Sliced fresh apples

Yield: 35 servings

Apricot Cheese Mousse

A welcome addition to a cocktail menu; the sweet taste offsets the usual tangy and salty offerings.

12 ounces cream cheese, softened

½ cup butter, softened

½ cup sour cream, at room temperature

½ cup sugar

1 envelope unflavored gelatin

¼ cup orange juice

1 cup chopped apricots

1 cup slivered almonds, toasted

Rind of 1 lemon, grated

Yield: 12 servings

Combine the cream cheese, butter, sour cream and sugar in a bowl; mix well.

Soften the gelatin in the orange juice in a saucepan. Cook over low heat until the gelatin is dissolved. Pour through a strainer. Add to the cheese mixture; blend well.

Fold in the apricots, almonds and lemon rind. Spoon into a 1-quart mold sprayed with nonstick cooking spray.

Chill until firm. Unmold onto a decorative plate. Serve with Swedish gingersnaps.

Black Bean Salsa Dip

Easy to make ahead and also to double, this sensational dip is great for a casual get-together.

Rinse and drain the black beans and place in a large bowl. Add the salsa, green onions, red pepper, lime juice, olive oil, garlic, cumin and cilantro; mix well.

Chill, covered, for 1 hour.

Fold in the avocado just before serving. Spoon the dip into a serving bowl and serve with tortilla chips.

Note: One teaspoon dried cilantro may be substituted for the fresh cilantro.

1 (15-ounce) can black beans
1 cup prepared salsa
¼ cup chopped green onions
¼ cup chopped red bell
   pepper
1 tablespoon lime juice
1 tablespoon olive oil
½ teaspoon minced garlic
¼ teaspoon ground cumin
2 tablespoons chopped fresh
   cilantro
1 avocado, chopped

Yield: 16 servings

Basil Mushrooms

These savory mushrooms will quickly disappear.

1 small onion, minced
2 cloves of garlic, minced
½ cup butter
1 pound fresh mushrooms
¼ cup chopped fresh or
1 teaspoon dried basil
1 teaspoon oregano
½ teaspoon thyme
½ teaspoon Tabasco sauce
2 tablespoons fresh lime juice
¼ cup dry sherry
½ teaspoon salt

Yield: 12 servings

Sauté the onion and garlic in the butter in a large skillet until tender. Add the mushrooms; coat well.

Add the basil, oregano, thyme, Tabasco sauce, lime juice, sherry and salt; mix well. Simmer, covered, until most of the liquid has evaporated. Serve in a chafing dish.

These mushrooms can be served not only as an appetizer but also as an accompaniment to beef or veal.

Crunchy Chicken Wings

*E*veryone will enjoy this alternative to the usual buffalo wings. Pretzels make them crunchy; the sauce makes them incredible. Provide plenty of napkins.

Preheat the oven to 350 degrees. Combine the butter, garlic powder and cayenne pepper in a bowl; blend well. Mix the pecans, pretzels and black pepper in a bowl; set aside.

Rinse the chicken and pat dry. Cut the chicken wings into 2 pieces at the joint, discarding the tips. Dip the chicken into the butter mixture. Roll in the pecan mixture to coat. Place on a greased baking sheet.

Bake at 350 degrees for 50 to 60 minutes or until golden brown. Place the chicken wings on a serving platter. Serve with the Chutney Pecan Sauce or Gourmet Hot Mustard for dipping. Garnish with sliced mangoes.

Chutney Pecan Sauce

Combine the butter, chutney, honey and pecans in a food processor container; process until the pecans are a chunky consistency. Spoon into a serving dish.

Gourmet Hot Mustard

Combine the sugar, vinegar, eggs, mustard and salt in a blender container. Process for 3 minutes. Pour into a double boiler over hot water. Cook for 4 to 6 minutes or until thickened, stirring constantly. Pour into jars.

Chill, covered, for 1 hour. Store in the refrigerator.

½ cup melted butter
¼ teaspoon garlic powder
1 teaspoon cayenne pepper
½ cup finely chopped pecans
1 cup finely crushed pretzels
¼ teaspoon black pepper
2 pounds chicken wings
Mangoes, peeled, sliced

Chutney Pecan Sauce
¼ cup butter, softened
⅓ cup chutney
¼ cup honey
¼ cup pecan halves

Gourmet Hot Mustard
1 cup sugar
1 cup vinegar
3 eggs
1 (1-ounce) can dry mustard
½ teaspoon salt

Yield: 20 servings

Chicken Champagnoise

Creamy and indulgent.

5 pounds boneless, skinless
chicken breasts
Flour for coating
Salt and pepper to taste
6 to 10 tablespoons butter
2 medium onions,
finely chopped
4 cloves of garlic, minced
2 cups Champagne
2 cups whipping cream

Yield: 24 servings

Preheat the oven to 350 degrees.

Rinse the chicken and pat dry. Chop into bite-size pieces. Coat the chicken in flour; season with salt and pepper.

Melt 4 tablespoons of the butter in a Dutch oven. Add the chicken in small batches. Cook until seared, adding additional butter as needed. Remove the chicken to a bowl.

Add 2 tablespoons of the butter to the Dutch oven. Sauté the onions and garlic in the butter until translucent; drain. Add the Champagne. Simmer until the liquid is reduced by one third. Stir in the whipping cream and chicken; mix well.

Bake, covered, at 350 degrees for 20 minutes. Adjust the seasonings.

Note: Any white wine may be substituted for the Champagne.

Olive Caviar Crostini

*R̶edolent of caviar, the delectable olive mixture
is a foil for the smooth goat cheese.
A party favorite.*

Place the goat cheese and the cream cheese in a food processor container; process until mixed. Combine the black olives, kalamata olives, garlic, onion, olive oil, Worcestershire sauce, lemon juice, lemon zest and pepper in a food processor container; process until the mixture is chopped.

Spread the cheese mixture on the toast rounds. Top with the olive mixture.

As a colorful variation, garnish with cherry tomatoes and green bell pepper slices. Serve at room temperature.

3 ounces goat cheese
*3 ounces cream cheese,
    softened*
*1 (4-ounce) can chopped
    black olives*
1 cup pitted kalamata olives
2 cloves of garlic
¼ cup chopped yellow onion
2 to 3 tablespoons olive oil
*1½ tablespoons
    Worcestershire sauce*
Juice of 1 to 2 lemons
1 teaspoon grated lemon zest
1 teaspoon pepper
*1 to 2 loaves French bread,
    cut into rounds, toasted*

Yield: 25 servings

Roasted Peppers with Herbed Goat Cheese

Roasted peppers are just right with cocktails. Selecting peppers of several colors adds interest.

1¼ pounds fresh mild goat
cheese, crumbled
(about 4 cups)
¼ cup chopped fresh chives
¼ cup chopped fresh parsley
2 cloves of garlic, minced
2 teaspoons chopped
fresh thyme
3 tablespoons chopped
fresh basil
Grated zest of 1 lemon
½ teaspoon freshly
ground pepper
Pinch of cayenne pepper
Whipping cream (optional)
6 large red bell peppers, cut
into halves, roasted
Fresh thyme sprigs

Yield: 36 servings

Combine the cheese, chives, parsley, garlic, thyme, basil, lemon zest and ground pepper in a bowl; mix well. Season with cayenne pepper. Add a small amount of cream if the cheese mixture is very stiff and difficult to mix.

Spread the cheese mixture onto the pepper halves; roll into cylinders lengthwise. Chill, covered, for several hours or until the filling is firm.

Cut each pepper roll crosswise into 6 rounds. Arrange on a serving platter; garnish with the thyme sprigs.

Note: To roast bell peppers, core and de-rib the peppers. Cut into large sections that will lay fairly flat, skin side up, on a broiling pan. Broil until the skin is dark brown and blistered. Place peppers immediately in an airtight container or plastic bag to steam. Let cool to room temperature; remove skin. Use in recipe or season with kosher salt, cracked pepper, and drizzle with olive oil.

Party Rosemary Pork

Serve with homemade rolls and a flavored mayonnaise that complements the rosemary without overpowering it.

Preheat the oven to 350 degrees. Place the pork loins side by side, fat side up, in a large heavy roasting pan. Roast the pork at 350 degrees for 30 minutes.

Mix the dried rosemary with the olive oil, pepper, vinegar and salt in a bowl. Spoon over the pork. Roast for about 30 minutes longer or to 160 to 165 degrees on a meat thermometer. Remove from the oven and cover loosely with foil. Let stand for 10 minutes.

Slice the pork thinly and arrange on serving platters. Garnish with rosemary sprigs. Serve on rolls warm or at room temperature.

Also delicious as a main course.

2 (3½-pound) rolled and tied
  boneless pork loins
¼ cup dried rosemary
¼ cup plus 2 tablespoons
  olive oil
2 tablespoons coarsely ground
  black pepper
2 tablespoons balsamic
  vinegar
2 teaspoons coarse (kosher)
  salt
Fresh rosemary sprigs

Yield: 25 servings

Stuffed New Potatoes

A surprisingly elegant turn on a classic dish. The potato salad alone is wonderful.

20 new potatoes
2 stalks celery, finely chopped
2 scallions, finely chopped
1 medium carrot,
finely chopped
2 hard-cooked eggs,
coarsely grated
2 tablespoons finely chopped
sweet gherkin pickles
2 tablespoons finely chopped
fresh dill
2 tablespoons chopped
Italian parsley
¾ teaspoon coarsely ground
black pepper
½ teaspoon salt
1 cup mayonnaise
1 cup sour cream

Yield: 40 servings

Boil the potatoes in enough water to cover in a large saucepan for 15 to 20 minutes or until tender. Drain and let stand until cool. Slice each potato into halves, cutting a slice off the round end of each half so each potato will stand upright. Scoop out the center of each potato half.

Combine the potato centers, celery, scallions, carrot, eggs, pickles, dill, parsley, pepper and salt in a bowl; mix gently.

Combine the mayonnaise and sour cream in a bowl. Fold in the potato mixture and mix gently. Spoon the potato salad into the potato shells.

Chill, covered, for 1 hour. Sprinkle with additional chopped fresh dill. Arrange on a decorative platter to serve.

Note: A small melon ball scoop works well for removing the centers of the potatoes.

Marinated Shrimp

*R*emove the shrimp from the marinade and present
on a lovely bed of varied lettuces.

Combine the celery, onions, capers, oil, vinegar, bay leaves, salt, pickling spice, celery seeds and Tabasco sauce in a bowl; mix well. Add the shrimp and coat well with the mixture.

Marinate, covered, in the refrigerator for 8 to 12 hours or longer. Drain and place on a lettuce-lined serving dish. Serve with assorted crackers.

½ cup thinly chopped celery tops
2 cups thinly sliced onions
2½ tablespoons undrained capers
1¼ cups vegetable oil
¾ cup white vinegar
7 to 8 bay leaves
4½ teaspoons salt
¼ cup pickling spice
2½ teaspoons celery seeds
Tabasco sauce to taste
2½ pounds cooked shrimp, peeled

Yield: 10 servings

Coconut Shrimp

Fried shrimp lovers—and that's almost everyone— will rave over this!

2 cups flour
½ teaspoon baking powder
½ teaspoon paprika
½ teaspoon curry powder
1 (12-ounce) can beer
2 pounds medium fresh shrimp
14 ounces flaked coconut
Orange marmalade
Horseradish

Yield: 12 servings

Combine 1½ cups flour, baking powder, paprika, curry powder and beer in a bowl; mix well.

Peel and devein the shrimp, leaving the tails. Coat the shrimp with ½ cup flour. Dip into the batter and roll in the coconut.

Preheat the oil in a deep fryer to 350 degrees. Deep-fry the shrimp until golden brown; drain. Serve warm with a sauce of orange marmalade mixed with a dash of horseradish.

Vidalia Onion Toast

Use only Vidalia onions—their sweetness is unequaled.

1 large Vidalia onion
1 cup mayonnaise
1 cup Parmesan cheese
2 French bread baguettes
Paprika to taste

Yield: 25 servings

Preheat the oven to 350 degrees.

Mince the onion. Combine the onion, mayonnaise and cheese in a bowl; mix well. Spread on the sliced bread. Sprinkle with paprika. Place on a baking sheet. Bake at 350 degrees for 10 minutes.

Smoked Salmon with Horseradish Sauce

Serve with thinly sliced white or pumpernickel bread.

Whip the whipping cream in a bowl. Squeeze the grated horseradish dry in a paper towel. Mix the horseradish with the lemon juice in a bowl. Fold into the whipped cream. Spoon into a serving bowl.

Chill for several hours. Serve cold with the salmon.

2 cups whipping cream
2 tablespoons freshly grated horseradish
Juice of ½ lemon
1 pound smoked salmon

Yield: 16 servings

Snow Peas Filled with Curried Chicken

This is beautiful as well as delicious—ideal for an afternoon wedding or tea.

Combine the mayonnaise, sour cream, curry powder and salt in a bowl; mix well. Chop the chicken into bite-size pieces. Add the chicken to the curry mixture, stirring gently.

Slice each snow pea along one seam edge and remove the peas. Place the pods in a colander and submerge in boiling water for 10 seconds. Plunge into ice water immediately; drain.

Fill each pod with 1 to 2 teaspoons of the curried chicken and place on a plate. Chill, covered, for 1 hour. Garnish each snow pea with a red bell pepper strip and arrange on a serving plate.

½ cup each mayonnaise and sour cream
1½ teaspoons curry powder
½ teaspoon salt
2 skinless, boneless chicken breasts, cooked
40 snow peas

Yield: 40 servings

Appetizers

Southern Vegetable Terrine

This colorful and impressive version of the classic French dish is made with traditionally Southern ingredients. At Huntsville's Green Bottle Grill, it is served with a cucumber and sun-dried tomato vinaigrette, accompanied by olives.

12 ounces boneless, skinless chicken breasts

2 egg whites

2 cups whipping cream

2 tablespoons chopped basil

1 teaspoon thyme

Salt and pepper to taste

3 carrots, julienned

2 yellow squash, cut into strips

1 zucchini, cut into strips

8 ounces okra, blanched and cut into strips

10 large collard leaves

6 artichoke hearts, cut into strips

1 tomato, peeled, seeded and julienned

Yield: 12 servings

Purée the chicken and the egg whites in a food processor. Add the cream slowly, processing constantly. Fold in the herbs, salt and pepper. Chill in the refrigerator.

Blanch the carrots, squash, zucchini, okra and collard leaves separately by submerging in boiling water for 2 to 3 minutes. Refresh by submerging in cold water to stop the cooking process.

Preheat the oven to 350 degrees.

Grease a paté mold or a loaf pan. Line the greased mold with collard leaves, allowing a 2 to 3 inch overlap over all edges. Alternate layers of the chicken mixture and vegetables in the prepared mold, beginning and ending with the chicken mixture. Fold overlapping collard leaves over the top.

Bake at 350 degrees in a water bath for 1 hour. Chill in the refrigerator. Invert to release the terrine onto a serving plate and slice to serve.

Blackberry Lemonade

Escape to a front porch swing on a lazy summer afternoon with this delicious lemonade.

Purée the blackberries in a food processor; strain. Add water, lemonade concentrate and sugar. Mix and chill for several hours. Serve over ice cubes and garnish with lemon slices and fresh mint.

3½ pints fresh blackberries
12 cups water
2 (12-ounce) cans frozen lemonade concentrate
3 tablespoons sugar

Yield: 12 servings

Backyard Frozen Fruit Cooler

With or without the vodka, making this frozen fruit drink on a warm summer day signals the entire family that games in the backyard will be forthcoming and friends are invited.

Combine the lemonade concentrate, vodka, strawberries and banana slices in a blender container. Add enough ice to cover the ingredients.

Process until smooth. Pour into serving cups.

Note: May substitute ginger ale for vodka.

1 (6-ounce) can frozen lemonade concentrate
1 concentrate can vodka
2 cups fresh strawberries
1 banana, sliced

Yield: 4 servings

Some-Like-It-Hot Bloody Marys

*P*ack a cooler with these delicious Bloody Marys for
your next tailgate party.

1 (46-ounce) can vegetable
juice cocktail
1 cup vodka
½ cup Worcestershire sauce
2 tablespoons barbecue sauce
Juice of ¼ lemon
Celery seeds and Tabasco
sauce to taste

Yield: 12 servings

Combine the vegetable juice, vodka, Worcestershire sauce,
barbecue sauce, lemon juice, celery seeds and Tabasco sauce in a
large pitcher; mix well.

Serve over crushed ice.

Peppermint Ice Cream Punch

*Y*ou'll be a popular parent when you serve Peppermint
Ice Cream Punch—a great choice for a child's party.

½ gallon vanilla ice cream
1 cup crushed soft peppermint
candy sticks
½ gallon chocolate milk

Yield: 12 servings

Place the ice cream and the candy in a medium punch
bowl. Pour the chocolate milk over the ice cream and candy.

Ladle into punch cups.

Mexican Hot Chocolate

Remember this recipe the next time you're really cold! Leave out the Kahlúa for a delicious hot chocolate the kids will love.

Combine the milk, brown sugar, cinnamon, vanilla and a dash of salt if desired in a large saucepan and mix well. Bring just to a boil over medium heat.

Whisk the chocolate and ½ cup of the hot milk mixture in a bowl until the chocolate melts. Add to the remaining milk mixture in the saucepan. Simmer for 2 minutes.

Stir in the Kahlúa and blend well. Pour into serving cups and serve with cinnamon sticks for stirring.

3½ cups milk
⅓ cup packed brown sugar
¾ teaspoon cinnamon
1½ teaspoons vanilla extract
3 ounces unsweetened
   chocolate, finely chopped
½ cup Kahlúa

Yield: 4 servings

Sparkling Cranberry Punch

This sophisticated, pretty and slightly tart punch appeals to those who like a not-too-sweet beverage.

Combine the orange juice, pineapple juice and cranberry juice in a large punch bowl and mix well.

Chill for 2 hours or longer.

Blend in the ginger ale just before serving. Place an ice ring in the punch bowl and garnish with orange slices.

4 cups orange juice
2 cups pineapple juice
6 cups cranberry juice
4 cups ginger ale

Yield: 32 servings

Beverages

Fresh Mint Tea

his is a delightful and refreshing choice for a warm-weather brunch or shower. A good non-alcoholic companion to Bloody Marys or mimosas.

4 quarts water
2 large (family-size) tea bags
Mint leaves to taste
1 cup sugar or to taste
1 (12-ounce) can each frozen orange juice and lemonade concentrate

Yield: 16 servings

Bring 4 cups of the water to a boil in a saucepan. Pour over the tea bags and mint leaves in a small pitcher. Steep for 10 minutes or longer; strain into a 1-gallon pitcher.

Add the sugar, orange juice concentrate and lemonade concentrate; stir until dissolved. Add the remaining water and mix well.

Note: May reduce the orange juice concentrate to one 6-ounce can and add one 6-ounce can pineapple juice concentrate.

Bridge over Tennessee River

Chip Cooper

*The Whitesburg Bridge spans the Tennessee River at Ditto Landing.
As in times past, the river brings beauty and provides recreation and
transportation to the North Alabama region.*

This photograph was underwritten by Mary Beasley Dean, President 1981–1982; Patsy Binkley Haws, President, 1987–1988

Photograph right:
By Guntersville Lake.
Heart-of-Dixie Slaw
Corn Santa Fe
Fried Tennessee River Catfish
Squash Puppies

Overleaf:
Green Salad with Pears
and Walnuts

Soups & Salads

❦

*I wish you were here in the
warm, sunny south today.
Little sister and I would take
you out into the garden,
and pick the delicious
raspberries and
a few strawberries for you.*

—Helen Keller
The Story of My Life

This photograph was underwritten by Sue Spragins Hill Fleming, President 1953–1954

Black Bean Soup

Add a tossed green salad and a loaf of French bread for a simple, savory dinner.

Bring the ham bone and water to a boil in a stockpot; reduce heat. Simmer, covered, for several hours. Strain, reserving 6 cups ham stock. Chill for 12 hours; skim. Remove the ham from the ham bone; chop coarsely. Combine the ham with additional chopped ham to equal 2 cups. Chill, covered, in the refrigerator.

Sort and rinse the black beans. Soak the beans overnight in enough water to cover; drain.

Sauté the onion, garlic, celery and chopped ham in a stockpot until the onion is tender. Stir in the black beans, reserved ham stock, carrots, red pepper, oregano and black pepper.

Cook, covered, over medium-low heat for 1 hour, stirring occasionally; reduce heat. Simmer, covered, for 3 to 12 hours or until the black beans are tender and the soup is of the desired consistency, stirring occasionally.

Ladle into soup bowls. Garnish with a dollop of sour cream and chopped green onions.

Traditionally served over white rice.

1 meaty ham bone
2 quarts water
Chopped ham (if needed)
1 (16-ounce) package dried
   black beans
1 large onion, chopped
4 cloves of garlic, crushed
2 cups chopped celery
2 carrots, grated
1 teaspoon crushed red
   pepper
1 tablespoon oregano
1 tablespoon freshly ground
   black pepper
Sour cream
Chopped green onions

Yield: 6 to 8 servings

Alabama Chicken Gumbo

cross between a gumbo and a Brunswick stew. Children will prefer this to a traditional hot and spicy gumbo. This recipe makes a large quantity; freeze half or share with friends.

1 (2½- to 3-pound) chicken or
3 whole chicken breasts
2 quarts water
1 cup chopped onion
1 cup chopped celery
1 tablespoon salt
1 teaspoon pepper
3 tablespoons melted
margarine
3 tablespoons flour
3 to 4 medium tomatoes,
peeled, chopped
4 cups fresh baby lima beans
4 cups (½-inch slices) okra
4 cups fresh corn kernels

Yield: 10 servings

Rinse the chicken. Combine the chicken, water, onion, celery, salt and pepper in a stockpot. Bring to a boil; reduce heat.

Simmer until the chicken is tender. Drain, reserving the broth and chicken. Chill the broth for 6 to 8 hours; skim. Chop the chicken, discarding the skin and bones.

Combine the margarine and flour in a stockpot; mix well. Cook over medium heat until golden brown, stirring constantly. Heat the reserved chicken broth in a saucepan until warm. Add the chicken broth 2 cups at a time to the roux, stirring until blended. Add the tomatoes, lima beans, okra, corn and chicken; mix well. Bring to a boil; reduce heat.

Simmer for 1 hour, stirring occasionally. Add additional chicken broth or water as needed for desired consistency; adjust seasonings. Ladle into soup bowls. Serve with cornbread, crusty French bread or ladle over rice.

Note: If time is of the essence, use canned chicken, chicken broth, tomatoes and frozen lima beans, okra and corn. May prepare in advance, refrigerate or freeze and reheat the day of serving.

Fiesta Chicken Soup

So comforting and delicious, your family will want seconds.

Rinse the chicken and pat dry. Cut into bite-size pieces. Sprinkle with the fajita seasoning mix. Sauté in olive oil in a skillet until brown; drain.

Process the corn, jalapeños, garlic and broth in a blender until puréed. Heat the butter in a saucepan until melted. Stir in the corn mixture, salt, cayenne pepper, oregano and undrained tomatoes. Add the cheese; mix well.

Cook over low heat for 10 minutes or until the cheese melts, stirring frequently. Remove from heat. Stir in the half-and-half. Ladle into soup bowls. Serve with crushed tortilla chips.

Note: For variety, serve with baked tortilla strips. To prepare tortilla strips, cut flour or corn tortillas into thin strips. Arrange on a baking sheet sprayed with nonstick cooking spray. Bake until crisp, turning several times.

1 pound skinless, boneless chicken breasts
1/2 envelope fajita seasoning mix
3 tablespoons olive oil
1 (17-ounce) can cream-style corn
2 jalapeños, seeded, finely chopped
3 to 5 garlic cloves, minced
1 cup chicken broth
1/4 cup butter
1/4 teaspoon salt
1/4 teaspoon cayenne pepper
1/2 teaspoon oregano
1 (16-ounce) can Mexican-style tomatoes, chopped
1 cup shredded Monterey Jack cheese
2 cups half-and-half
Tortilla chips

Yield: 10 to 12 servings

Lentil Soup with Italian Sausage

Everyone is rediscovering lentils—and with good reason. They're high in fiber, inexpensive and delicious. Once you make this soup, you'll prepare it often.

1 (16-ounce) package lentils
1½ pounds Italian sausage
1 large onion, chopped
3 cloves of garlic, crushed
6 cups water
3 carrots, sliced
6 beef bouillon cubes
2 tablespoons oregano
¼ cup chopped fresh parsley
1 teaspoon salt
Freshly ground pepper to taste
1 (10-ounce) package frozen chopped spinach, thawed
Grated Parmesan cheese

Yield: 6 to 8 servings

Sort and rinse the lentils. Combine with enough water to cover in a bowl. Soak for 3 hours or longer; drain.

Brown the sausage with the onion and garlic in a stockpot, stirring until the sausage is crumbly; drain. Stir in the lentils, 6 cups water, carrots, bouillon cubes, oregano, parsley, salt and pepper; cover.

Bring to a boil; reduce heat. Simmer for 1 hour, stirring occasionally. Stir in the spinach. Simmer for 2 hours, stirring occasionally.

Ladle into soup bowls; sprinkle with the cheese.

Prepare 1 day in advance to enhance the flavor. May freeze for future use.

Chunky Gazpacho

azpacho is just too good to be so low in fat. Show off your fresh garden vegetables in this zesty summer staple.

Mash the garlic, salt, wine vinegar, olive oil and bread in a bowl until of paste consistency.

Combine the tomatoes, green pepper, cucumbers, celery, radishes, onion, parsley and tomato juice in a large bowl; mix well. Stir in the garlic mixture. Season with salt and pepper.

Chill, covered, for 12 hours. Ladle into chilled soup bowls. Garnish with parsley sprigs and nonfat yogurt. Serve with croutons. May add Tabasco sauce for a spicier soup.

Note: To seed cucumbers, cut into halves lengthwise and remove seeds with a teaspoon. To seed tomatoes, cut into halves crosswise and squeeze to remove seeds.

4 cloves of garlic

1 teaspoon salt

2 tablespoons red wine vinegar

3 tablespoons olive oil

1 cup trimmed French bread pieces

4 tomatoes, peeled, seeded, chopped

1 green bell pepper, chopped

2 cucumbers, peeled, seeded, chopped

1/2 cup chopped celery

1/2 cup chopped white radishes

1/4 cup chopped red onion

2 tablespoons finely chopped fresh parsley

2 cups tomato juice

Salt and pepper to taste

Parsley sprigs

Nonfat yogurt

Croutons

Tabasco sauce (optional)

Yield: 8 servings

Oyster Artichoke Bisque

A perfect first course for a romantic dinner. For a Valentine's Day menu follow this with a simple meat or chicken dish and something chocolate for dessert.

24 oysters with liquid

2 (14-ounce) cans quartered artichoke hearts, drained

2 quarts chicken stock

1 cup sliced green onions

1 tablespoon chopped fresh parsley

1 teaspoon salt

1 teaspoon thyme

Cayenne pepper to taste

1½ cups melted butter

1½ cups flour

2 cups whipping cream

Green onions for garnish

Yield: 8 servings

Bring the oysters and liquid, artichokes, chicken stock, green onions, parsley, salt, thyme and cayenne pepper to a boil in a stockpot, stirring occasionally.

Melt the butter in a small saucepan and blend in the flour. Add to the oyster mixture; mix well. Stir in the whipping cream; reduce heat.

Simmer for 10 minutes, stirring frequently. Ladle into soup bowls. Garnish with additional chopped green onions.

Fresh Blueberry Soup

ote that this light, fruity soup has no fat. For an unusual dessert, forget the calories and top with whipped cream and blueberries.

Combine the blueberries, grape juice, 1 cup water, cinnamon stick and sugar in a saucepan; mix well. Bring to a boil; reduce heat.

Simmer, covered, for 5 minutes, stirring occasionally. Stir in a mixture of cornstarch and 1/4 cup water. Add the cardamom; mix well.

Cook until thickened, stirring constantly. Remove from heat. Let stand until cool.

Store, covered, in the refrigerator until chilled. Discard the cinnamon stick. Ladle into soup bowls.

1½ cups fresh blueberries
1¼ cups unsweetened grape juice
1 cup water
1 (3-inch) cinnamon stick
2 teaspoons sugar
2 tablespoons cornstarch
¼ cup water
⅛ teaspoon cardamom

Yield: 4 servings

Eggplant and Sweet Pepper Purée

An extraordinary soup for special occasions.

Chive Crèam Fraîche
½ bunch chives, sliced
Juice of 1 lemon
1 cup whipping cream
Salt and white pepper to taste

**Eggplant and
Sweet Pepper Purée**
2 medium onions, chopped
2 stalks celery, chopped
2 carrots, chopped
2 tablespoons olive oil
*1 tablespoon each minced
shallots and garlic*
*2 medium eggplant,
peeled, chopped*
*1 each red and yellow bell
pepper, chopped*
*2 quarts homemade chicken
stock, skimmed*
Bouquet garni
Hot pepper sauce to taste
½ teaspoon salt
¼ teaspoon black pepper
1 cup whipping cream
½ cup butter, softened

Yield: 6 to 8 servings

For Chive Crèam Fraîche, pulverize half the chives with the lemon juice in a stainless steel bowl. Stir in 1 cup whipping cream. Chill for 1 hour or until thickened; strain. Stir in the remaining chives. Season with salt and white pepper to taste. Chill, covered, until serving time.

Eggplant and Sweet Pepper Purée

Sauté the onions, celery and carrots in the olive oil in a stockpot until tender. Add the shallots and garlic; mix well.

Cook until the garlic gives off an aroma, stirring constantly. Stir in the eggplant and bell peppers. Cook, tightly covered, for 10 minutes; do not brown. Add the chicken stock, bouquet garni, hot pepper sauce, ½ teaspoon salt and black pepper; mix well. Bring to a boil; reduce heat.

Simmer for 30 minutes, stirring occasionally. Remove bouquet garni. Process mixture in a blender just until puréed. Return to stockpot. Bring to a boil. Stir in the 1 cup whipping cream and butter. Cook just until heated through, stirring constantly.

Ladle into warm soup bowls. Top with the Chive Crème Fraîche and additional sliced chives.

Note: Make a bouquet garni of parsley, thyme, 2 bay leaves and 8 peppercorns tied in a cheesecloth bag.

Cold Peach Soup

It's your choice. Serve this fresh-tasting cold soup as an elegant first course, as a quick summer main dish or even as an unusual dessert.

Process the peaches in a food processor until puréed. Combine the peaches, orange juice, buttermilk, yogurt, cinnamon, cloves and allspice in a bowl; mix well.

Chill, covered, until serving time. Ladle into soup bowls. Garnish with additional sliced peaches, toasted almonds and fresh mint.

2 pounds peaches, peeled, coarsely chopped
½ cup frozen orange juice concentrate
1 cup buttermilk
1 cup plain yogurt
⅛ teaspoon cinnamon
⅛ teaspoon ground cloves
⅛ teaspoon ground allspice
Additional sliced peaches for garnish
Toasted almonds
Fresh mint

Yield: 6 to 8 servings

Cream of Tomato Soup

*W*hen fresh tomatoes are not at their peak, substitute canned tomatoes. This velvety soup will still be wonderful.

1 large onion, thinly sliced
½ teaspoon thyme
½ teaspoon basil
Salt and freshly ground
pepper to taste
½ cup butter
2 tablespoons olive oil
3 tablespoons tomato paste
2½ pounds ripe tomatoes,
peeled, cored
¼ cup flour
3¾ cups chicken broth
1 teaspoon sugar
1 cup whipping cream
¼ cup butter

Yield: 8 servings

Sauté the onion, thyme, basil, salt and pepper in a mixture of ½ cup butter and olive oil in a saucepan until the onion is tender. Add the tomato paste and tomatoes; mix well. Simmer for 10 minutes, stirring occasionally.

Combine the flour and 5 tablespoons of the chicken broth in a bowl; mix well. Stir into the tomato mixture. Add the remaining chicken broth; mix well.

Simmer for 30 minutes, stirring frequently. Process mixture in several batches in a food processor until smooth. Return to saucepan. Stir in the sugar and cream.

Simmer for 5 minutes, stirring frequently. Swirl in ¼ cup butter. Ladle into soup bowls.

Note: May substitute two 16-ounce cans Italian-style tomatoes for fresh tomatoes.

Cream of Watercress Soup

*M*adison County was once known as the "Watercress Capital of the World" because of the abundance of the watercress in the area's many springs. The slightly peppery taste of watercress makes a perfect rich, cream soup in the Huntsville tradition.

Trim and rinse the watercress; drain. Reserve several leaves for garnish.

Sauté the onion in the butter in a saucepan for 10 minutes or until tender. Add the watercress; sprinkle with ¼ teaspoon salt.

Cook, covered, over medium-low heat for 5 to 10 minutes or until the watercress is wilted. Stir in the flour.

Cook for 5 minutes, stirring occasionally. Add the boiling stock; mix well. Cook for 5 minutes. Process mixture in food processor until puréed.

Reheat the puréed mixture to a simmer in a saucepan just before serving. Beat the egg yolks and cream in a bowl until blended. Add the puréed mixture gradually into the egg mixture, whisking constantly until blended. Return the mixture to the saucepan. Heat, but do not allow to simmer, stirring constantly. Season with salt and pepper to taste. Ladle into soup bowls. Top with the reserved watercress.

May prepare 1 day in advance and serve chilled.

2 bunches watercress or spinach
¼ cup minced onion
2 tablespoons butter
¼ teaspoon salt
2 tablespoons flour
4 cups boiling chicken stock
2 egg yolks
1 cup whipping cream
Salt and pepper to taste

Yield: 6 servings

Mushroom and Wild Rice Soup

An *intricately flavored rich soup.*

4 ounces wild rice, rinsed
2 beef bouillon cubes
2½ cups water
1 medium onion, chopped
2 stalks celery, chopped
2 cloves of garlic, minced
2 tablespoons butter
1 pound fresh mushrooms,
sliced
½ cup sherry
½ teaspoon each of paprika,
salt, white pepper and
dry mustard
¼ teaspoon each of nutmeg
and allspice
1 to 2 teaspoons parsley
1 (14-ounce) can beef broth
2 cups half-and-half
2 cups shredded Monterey
Jack cheese
½ cup flour
1 cup hot water
Shredded Cheddar cheese
and Monterey Jack
cheese to taste

Yield: 4 servings

Bring the wild rice, bouillon cubes and 2½ cups water to a boil in a saucepan; reduce heat to medium. Cook for 45 to 60 minutes or until the water is absorbed.

Sauté the onion, celery and garlic in the butter in a stockpot until tender. May add a small amount of water to prevent vegetables from sticking. Stir in the mushrooms.

Sauté for 1 minute. Add the sherry; mix well. Stir in the paprika, salt, white pepper, dry mustard, nutmeg, allspice and parsley. Add the broth, half-and-half and 2 cups Monterey Jack cheese; mix well.

Cook over medium heat just until heated through, stirring constantly; do not boil. Stir in a mixture of flour and 1 cup hot water. Add the wild rice; mix well.

Simmer for 10 to 20 minutes or until of the desired consistency, stirring occasionally. Ladle into soup bowls. Sprinkle with a mixture of Cheddar cheese and Monterey Jack cheese to taste.

Elk River Brunswick Stew

runswick stew is always satisfying and flavorful. Serve with cornbread and your favorite coleslaw.

Rinse the chicken. Combine the chicken and water in a stockpot. Cook until the chicken is tender. Drain, reserving 2 quarts of the broth. Strain the broth. Chop the chicken, discarding the skin and bones.

Process the tomatoes, onions and 1 cup of the reserved broth in a food processor until ground.

Brown the ground chuck and sausage in a skillet, stirring until crumbly; drain. Combine with the remaining reserved chicken broth in the stockpot; mix well. Stir in the corn, potatoes, tomato mixture and chicken. Add the tomato sauce, tomato paste, catsup, hot sauce, garlic powder, salt and pepper; mix well.

Cook over low heat for 3 to 4 hours or until of the desired consistency, stirring occasionally. Ladle into soup bowls.

5 pounds chicken pieces
2½ quarts water
2 (16-ounce) cans tomatoes, drained
5 medium onions, chopped
1½ pounds ground chuck
1 pound hot sausage
2 (16-ounce) cans whole kernel corn, drained
6 medium potatoes, peeled, chopped
1 (15-ounce) can tomato sauce
1 (6-ounce) can tomato paste
1¾ cups catsup
1 tablespoon hot sauce
½ teaspoon garlic powder
4 teaspoons salt
1 teaspoon (heaping) pepper

Yield: 12 servings

Spicy White Chili

Consider Spicy White Chili for a casual winter get-together. Let your guests choose from toppings such as sour cream, chopped green onions, shredded Cheddar or Monterey Jack cheese, chopped tomatoes and tortilla strips.

1 (16-ounce) package dried white beans

6 cups chicken broth

2 medium onions, finely chopped

1 tablespoon vegetable oil

4 cups chopped cooked chicken

8 ounces garbanzo beans, cooked

3 (4-ounce) cans chopped green chiles, drained

2 teaspoons cumin

2 cloves of garlic, minced

1½ teaspoons oregano

1 teaspoon cayenne pepper

Yield: 6 to 8 servings

Sort and rinse the white beans. Combine the beans with enough water to cover in a stockpot. Soak for 12 hours; drain. Cook using package directions; drain.

Process 1 cup of the white beans in a blender until puréed. Combine the bean purée with the chicken broth in a stockpot; mix well. Cook over low heat until thickened.

Sauté the onions in the oil in a skillet; drain. Stir the onions into the bean mixture. Add the remaining white beans, chicken, garbanzo beans, green chiles, cumin, garlic, oregano and cayenne pepper; mix well.

Simmer for 2 hours, stirring occasionally. Ladle into soup bowls. Offer a choice of toppings.

Note: Canned white beans may be substituted for dried.

Stew in a Pumpkin

Of course, you don't have to serve this simple stew in a pumpkin—but it certainly is fun and festive.

Rinse pumpkin and pat dry. Slice top from pumpkin, reserving top; discard seeds and membranes. Brush inside with melted butter. Place the pumpkin in a round baking dish.

Sauté the onion, garlic and beef chuck in the oil in a stockpot until the onion and garlic are tender and the beef chuck is brown; drain. Add the tomatoes, sweet potatoes, Irish potatoes, broth, honey, salt and pepper; mix well. Cook, covered, over low heat for 2 hours, stirring occasionally. Stir in the corn. Cook, covered, for 20 minutes, stirring occasionally. May chill, covered, at this point for 12 hours to enhance flavor.

Preheat oven to 350 degrees. Pour the stew into the pumpkin; replace the top. Bake at 350 degrees for 1 hour; do not overcook as pumpkin will lose its shape.

1 pumpkin
¼ cup (or less) melted butter
1 large onion, coarsely chopped
2 cloves of garlic, minced
2 pounds beef chuck, cut into bite-size pieces
3 tablespoons vegetable oil
2 tomatoes, chopped
2 medium sweet potatoes, peeled, chopped
2 medium Irish potatoes, peeled, chopped
2 cups beef broth
1 tablespoon honey
Salt and pepper to taste
1½ cups cooked corn, at room temperature

Yield: 18 servings

It grows in a dazzling ample land
Of measureless breadth and room—
And the wealth of a splendid
tropical sun
Dowers this cotton bloom.

Maria Howard Weeden
The Cotton Bloom

This photograph was underwritten by Sallie B. Kelly Cobb, President 1967–1968

Soups

Sautéed Apple Salad

A splendid salad with just the right combination of flavors. Bleu cheese and walnuts are made for each other.

¼ cup red wine vinegar
1 tablespoon chopped
fresh thyme
½ cup plus 2 tablespoons
olive oil
Salt and pepper to taste
5 medium Granny Smith
apples, peeled, sliced
1 tablespoon sugar
6 cups torn young
lettuce leaves
1 cup crumbled bleu cheese
½ cup chopped toasted
walnuts

Yield: 6 servings

Combine the vinegar and thyme in a small bowl. Add ½ cup of the olive oil gradually, whisking constantly until blended. Season with salt and pepper. Set aside.

Sauté the apples and sugar in the remaining 2 tablespoons oil in a large skillet over medium-high heat until the apples are slightly tender. Cool.

Arrange the lettuce in a large salad bowl; layer the apple mixture over the top. Sprinkle with the bleu cheese and walnuts. Add the oil and vinegar dressing, tossing gently to coat.

Corn Santa Fe

A colorful dish for a casual dinner. Make ahead and let the flavors blend—this dish is ready when you are.

Bring water to a boil in a stockpot. Add the corn. Cook for 10 minutes or until water returns to a boil; drain. Rinse with cold water. Cut the corn off the cob.

Combine the avocado, corn, olives, red pepper, almonds, green onions, garlic, pepper, oregano, olive oil, lemon juice and vinegar in a large bowl; mix well.

Serve on lettuce leaves, red cabbage or corn shucks.

Note: Add a small amount of lemon juice and sugar to the boiling water when cooking corn to enhance the flavor.

8 ears of fresh corn
1 ripe avocado, peeled, chopped
1 (2-ounce) can sliced black olives, drained
1 chopped red bell pepper
2 tablespoons slivered almonds, toasted
2 tablespoons chopped green onions
2 cloves of garlic, minced
1/4 teaspoon ground pepper
2 to 3 teaspoons fresh oregano or 1 teaspoon dried oregano
3 tablespoons extra-virgin olive oil
1 tablespoon lemon juice
2 tablespoons white wine vinegar

Yield: 6 servings

Green Salad with Pears and Walnuts

In this simple but sophisticated salad, sweet pears and tart dressing are a winning combination.

1 head romaine lettuce

1 small head radicchio

¼ cup chopped walnuts, toasted

½ to 1 cup shaved Parmesan cheese

2 pears

Creamy Herb Salad Dressing

1 egg yolk

1 tablespoon Dijon mustard

¼ cup fresh lemon juice

2 tablespoons tarragon vinegar

1 tablespoon dried tarragon

¾ cup vegetable oil

1 cup olive oil

Salt and freshly ground pepper to taste

Yield: 6 servings

Rinse the romaine lettuce and radicchio. Separate into leaves. Chill, wrapped in paper towels, allowing to dry thoroughly.

Tear the romaine lettuce and radicchio into bite-size pieces. Combine with the walnuts in a salad bowl; mix well. Add the Parmesan cheese. Peel and slice the pears just before serving. Add to the salad; mix well.

Toss the salad with just enough of the Creamy Herb Salad Dressing to coat. Serve immediately.

Note: For shaved Parmesan cheese, scrape the cheese with a vegetable peeler.

Creamy Herb Salad Dressing

Whisk the egg yolk and mustard in a medium bowl until blended. Add the lemon juice, vinegar and tarragon; mix well. Add the vegetable oil and olive oil in a fine stream, whisking constantly until blended. Season with salt and pepper. Store, in a covered jar, in the refrigerator.

Note: Egg yolk may omitted; the dressing will not be as creamy but makes a nice vinaigrette.

Chicken Pasta Salad

A great basic with a spicy flavor, this dish will receive rave reviews.

Sprinkle the chicken with vinegar and salt in a bowl. Chill, covered, for 8 hours.

Cook the pasta in boiling water in a saucepan using package directions; drain. Toss with the olive oil. Set aside.

Combine the chicken, pasta, celery, bell pepper, green onions and pimento in a large bowl. Add the Creole Mayonnaise; toss to coat. Chill, covered, for 2 hours or longer.

Serve the chicken and pasta over a bed of lettuce on a serving platter.

Note: May be prepared 1 day in advance of serving.

Creole Mayonnaise

Combine the mayonnaise, dill weed, black pepper, celery seeds, parsley, Creole seasoning and lemon juice in a bowl; mix well.

4 whole chicken breasts, cooked, chopped
¼ cup balsamic vinegar
1½ teaspoons salt
1 (16-ounce) package rotini
1 tablespoon olive oil
1 cup chopped celery
½ cup chopped bell pepper
3 tablespoons chopped green onions
2 tablespoons chopped pimento

Creole Mayonnaise
1 cup mayonnaise
½ teaspoon dill weed
⅛ teaspoon ground black pepper
½ teaspoon celery seeds
½ cup chopped parsley
1 teaspoon Creole seasoning
2 teaspoons lemon juice

Yield: 10 servings

Curried Seafood Salad

The key is the exotic dressing.

1 pound peeled, cooked shrimp
1 pound crabmeat
1 red bell pepper, chopped
1 yellow bell pepper, chopped
8 mint leaves, chopped
¼ cup currants
1 stalk celery, chopped
1 (16 ounce) package pasta shells, cooked, drained

Curry Dressing
1 cup mayonnaise
2 tablespoons sour cream
2 tablespoons lime juice
2 tablespoons mango chutney
2 tablespoons curry powder
1 tablespoon (or more) milk

Yield: 12 servings

Combine the shrimp and crabmeat in a large bowl. Add the bell peppers, mint leaves, currants and celery and mix gently. Stir in the pasta shells.

Add the chilled Curry Dressing to the shrimp mixture just before serving, tossing to coat.

Curry Dressing

Combine the mayonnaise, sour cream, lime juice, chutney and curry powder in a small bowl. Add the milk, stirring until of the desired consistency.

Chill, covered, until serving time.

Grilled Shrimp and Sweet Pepper Salad

*D*on't overcook the shrimp. When they
turn pink, they're done.

Mix the garlic and basil leaves with the olive oil in a medium bowl. Add the parsley. Add the shrimp, tossing to coat. Marinate, covered, in the refrigerator for 3 hours.

Combine the bell peppers and onion in a medium bowl; set aside.

Grill the shrimp over hot coals until the shrimp turn pink. Toss with the bell pepper mixture. Add the Balsamic Vinaigrette, tossing to coat. Let stand for 30 minutes before serving.

Balsamic Vinaigrette

Combine the shallots, parsley, basil and balsamic vinegar in a small bowl. Add the olive oil in a fine stream, whisking constantly. Season with salt and pepper; set aside.

20 cloves of garlic, lightly
   crushed
10 basil leaves, chopped
2 tablespoons olive oil
Sprigs of fresh parsley to taste
1 pound medium shrimp,
   peeled, deveined
4 red bell peppers, thinly
   sliced
4 yellow bell peppers, thinly
   sliced
1 red onion, sliced

Balsamic Vinaigrette
2 tablespoons chopped
   shallots
Chopped parsley and basil to
   taste
¼ cup balsamic vinegar
1 cup extra-virgin olive oil
Salt and pepper to taste

Yield: 4 servings

Steak Salad with Pepper Dressing

Prepare the lettuce and dressing while the grill readies; add the sliced steak warm from the coals. A red wine and French bread complete a romantic dinner.

½ cup soy sauce

6 tablespoons sugar

1 tablespoon grated ginger

1 (12-ounce) New York top loin steak, 1-inch thick

2 cups torn escarole

2 cups torn radicchio

2 cups torn Boston lettuce

2 cups torn red leaf lettuce

¼ English cucumber, julienned

1⅓ cups thinly sliced red onion

1 teaspoon black sesame seeds

12 fresh cilantro sprigs

Pepper Dressing

¼ cup soy sauce

2 tablespoons fresh lemon juice

¾ teaspoon minced jalapeño

2 tablespoons peanut oil

2 tablespoons olive oil

Yield: 4 servings

Combine ½ cup soy sauce, sugar and grated ginger in a shallow dish, stirring until the sugar dissolves. Add the steak, turning to coat. Chill, covered, for 2 hours, turning the steak occasionally.

Preheat the grill.

Toss the escarole, radicchio, Boston lettuce and red leaf lettuce in a large salad bowl. Add the cucumber and red onion; set aside.

Drain the steak. Grill over hot coals for 3 minutes per side for rare or to the desired degree of doneness.

Toss the greens with the Pepper Dressing until coated. Arrange the salad on 4 salad plates. Slice the steak thinly across the grain; arrange on top of the salad. Sprinkle with the sesame seeds. Top with the cilantro.

Pepper Dressing

Whisk ¼ cup soy sauce, lemon juice and jalapeño in a small bowl. Add the peanut oil and olive oil gradually, whisking constantly until blended.

Broccoli and Red Grape Salad

You'll be surprised at how well the sweet sauce and red grapes complement the broccoli. This is a delicious salad for lunch in the summertime.

Combine the broccoli, grapes, onion, sunflower nuts and bacon in a large salad bowl; mix well.

Mix the mayonnaise, sugar and vinegar in a small bowl. Add to the broccoli mixture, tossing to coat. Chill, covered, until serving time.

Note: May substitute raisins for the grapes.

1 bunch fresh broccoli, cut into bite-size pieces
2 cups chopped red grapes
½ red onion, chopped
1 cup shelled sunflower seeds
12 slices crisp-fried bacon, crumbled
1 cup mayonnaise
½ cup sugar
2 tablespoons vinegar

Yield: 12 servings

Heart-of-Dixie Slaw

This is a good hot-weather slaw without mayonnaise that travels well. Make it the night before and pack it to take on your next picnic.

1 head cabbage, shredded
1 teaspoon salt
1½ cups sugar
1 cup vinegar
½ cup water
½ bunch of celery, chopped
1 green bell pepper, chopped
½ teaspoon celery seeds
1 purple onion, sliced,
separated into rings
1 (2-ounce) jar chopped
pimento
½ teaspoon mustard seeds

Yield: 6 servings

Combine the cabbage and salt in a bowl; mix well. Let stand for 1 hour. Squeeze moisture from the cabbage.

Bring the sugar, vinegar and water to a boil in a medium saucepan. Boil for 2 minutes. Let stand until cool.

Combine the celery, bell pepper, celery seeds, onion, pimento, mustard seeds and cabbage in a medium bowl; mix well. Pour the vinegar mixture over the cabbage mixture, tossing gently to coat.

Chill, covered, until serving time.

Cucumber Mousse

*Cool as a cucumber and a refreshing accompaniment
to a spicy main course.*

Dissolve the gelatin in the boiling water in a small bowl. Stir in the lime juice. Let stand until cool.

Peel the cucumbers and slice lengthwise; remove the seeds. Grate the cucumbers into a strainer; drain.

Process the cottage cheese in a food processor until creamy. Add the salt, onion, cucumbers and gelatin mixture; mix well. Stir in the mayonnaise.

Spoon into a salad mold. Chill until set.

Unmold onto a serving plate. Sprinkle with the toasted almonds before serving. Garnish with sliced cucumbers and tomato wedges.

*3 (3-ounce) packages lime
    gelatin*
1½ cups boiling water
Juice of 2 limes
3 large cucumbers
2 cups cottage cheese
Salt to taste
1 large onion, chopped
2 cups mayonnaise
1 cup sliced almonds, toasted

Yield: 8 servings

Wilted Romaine Salad

*If you like Caesar salads, you'll love
this warm variation.*

6 cups bite-size pieces
romaine lettuce
½ cup chopped mushrooms
2 tablespoons red wine
vinegar
1 teaspoon anchovy paste
1 large red onion, chopped
6 tablespoons olive oil
1⅓ cups toasted croutons
Freshly ground black pepper
to taste

Yield: 6 servings

Combine the lettuce and mushrooms in a glass or ceramic salad bowl; set aside.

Beat the vinegar and anchovy paste in a small mixer bowl until smooth; set aside.

Sauté the onion in the olive oil in a large skillet over medium-high heat just until wilted. Add the croutons, tossing a few times to coat. Remove from heat. Stir in the vinegar mixture.

Pour the dressing over the lettuce mixture, tossing gently to coat. Season with the pepper. Toss and serve immediately.

Tomato and Onion Salad

So good when you have fresh-from-the-garden tomatoes and onions. It's an old Southern trick to soak the onions in ice water and drain well for a crisper, sweeter taste.

Whisk the vinegar, salt, pepper, garlic, parsley and basil in a large bowl. Add the oil in a fine stream, whisking constantly until mixed. Add the onions and tomatoes, tossing to coat.

Chill, covered, for 3 hours or longer. Garnish with basil leaves. Serve chilled.

½ cup red wine vinegar

1 teaspoon salt

½ teaspoon pepper

1 clove of garlic, crushed

1 to 2 tablespoons chopped fresh parsley

2 teaspoons dried basil

⅔ cup olive oil

2 red onions, sliced

4 large tomatoes, sliced

Yield: 6 servings

Tomato Aspic with Dill Mayonnaise

Tomato aspic is a standard for Southern summers. Serve it alone as a light lunch or as a complement to a pasta, chicken or seafood salad.

2 envelopes unflavored gelatin

¼ cup cold water

½ cup boiling water

4 cups vegetable juice cocktail

1 tablespoon minced dried onion

1 teaspoon sugar

1 teaspoon seasoned salt

2 bay leaves

1 teaspoon Worcestershire sauce

2 whole cloves

1 teaspoon salt

Juice of 1 lemon

Fresh vegetables of choice

Dill Mayonnaise

½ to ¾ cup mayonnaise

Dill weed to taste

Salt to taste

Garlic powder to taste

Yield: 10 servings

Soften the gelatin in the cold water for 5 minutes. Dissolve the gelatin in the boiling water; set aside.

Bring the vegetable juice cocktail, onion, sugar, seasoned salt, bay leaves, Worcestershire sauce, cloves and salt to a boil in a large saucepan; reduce heat. Simmer for 15 minutes.

Strain the juice mixture into a large bowl; stir in the lemon juice and gelatin. Pour into a 10-inch ring mold. Chill until partially set.

Chop the fresh vegetables such as cucumbers, radishes, celery or bell peppers in a food processor; drain. Add to the partially set aspic. Chill until set.

Invert the aspic onto a serving plate. Serve sliced with the Dill Mayonnaise.

Dill Mayonnaise

Combine the mayonnaise, dill weed, salt and garlic powder in a small bowl; mix well. Chill until ready to serve.

Vinaigrette with Pecans

A flavorful dressing that brings out the best in a mixed green or citrus salad.

Chop the shallots and pecans in a food processor. Add the vinegar, sugar, salt, white pepper and mustard, processing until smooth. Add the olive oil in a fine stream, processing constantly until blended.

Serve over a green salad topped with grapefruit sections and chopped avocado.

Note: May substitute walnuts for the pecans.

2 shallots
¼ cup pecans, toasted
3 tablespoons balsamic vinegar
1 teaspoon each sugar and salt
½ teaspoon white pepper
1 teaspoon Dijon mustard
1 cup extra-virgin olive oil

Yield: 1½ cups

Roquefort Salad Dressing

Delicious on salads, baked potatoes, crudités or chips. You will love this classic dressing on almost anything.

Crumble the cheese. Combine with sour cream, mayonnaise and pepper in a bowl, stirring until combined but chunky. Stir in the milk, thinning until of the desired consistency.

Store in the refrigerator for up to 2 weeks.

Note: May substitute bleu cheese for the Roquefort cheese, adding 1 teaspoon wine vinegar and garlic salt to taste. Use low-fat sour cream if desired.

8 ounces Roquefort cheese at room temperature
¾ cup each sour cream and mayonnaise
Freshly ground pepper to taste
1 tablespoon (or more) milk

Yield: 2 cups

Salads

Herb Vinegars

$\mathcal{H}$erb vinegars are beautiful and add flavor to any recipe that calls for vinegar. Use them in salad dressings and marinades, or on steamed vegetables or to deglaze a pan. These make lovely gifts.

White, cider, red wine, white wine or rice vinegar
Sprigs or leaves of fresh herbs such as dill, sweet basil, red basil, globe basil, coriander, rosemary, tarragon, parsley or thyme

Heat the vinegar in a saucepan until warm. Add a generous portion of fresh herb sprigs and leaves to a glass bottle. Pour in the warm vinegar. Cork the bottle.

Let stand at room temperature for 2 weeks before using.

Some good combinations to try are any of the basils in cider or red wine vinegar; dill, chives, oregano, rosemary or thyme in cider, white or white wine vinegar; rosemary sprigs, 2 peeled garlic cloves, a banana pepper, 2 red chile peppers and 1 tablespoon black peppercorns in white or cider vinegar.

Neighbors bring food with death and flowers with sickness and little things in between.

Harper Lee
To Kill a Mockingbird

Sweet Home Alabama

Spool and Store

Chip Cooper

Leaving the streets of downtown Huntsville to enter Harrison Brothers' hardware store, one crosses a threshold back into time. Founded in 1879, and in continuous operation at its present location since 1897, Harrison Brothers is the oldest hardware store in Alabama.

This photograph was underwritten by Jane Walker Troup, President 1976–1977; Jeanne Luther McCown, President, 1969–1970

Photograph right:
Tenderloin Stuffed with Lobster

Overleaf:
Pan-Roasted Rabbit with Linguini
Grilled Quail with
Black-Eyed Pea Salad
Skillet Apple Tart with
Calvados Cream

Main Courses

Next morning it was I who
waked the whole family with my
first "Merry Christmas!"
I found surprises,
not in the stocking only,
but on the table . . .

—Helen Keller
The Story of My Life

Filet of Beef en Croûte

A beautiful presentation. Use frozen puff pastry if you like—good commercial puff pastry is an excellent shortcut.

Preheat the oven to 450 degrees. Roll the Pastry into a rectangle large enough to enclose the tenderloin on a lightly floured surface.

Spread with the sausage; sprinkle with the mushrooms. Arrange the tenderloin over the prepared layers. Fold the Pastry over the tenderloin, enclosing completely; fold the ends.

Cut a penny-size hole in the top. Brush with a mixture of egg yolk and 1 tablespoon water. Place on a baking sheet.

Bake at 450 degrees for 45 minutes.

Pastry

Cut the butter into the flour in a bowl until crumbly. Stir in the ½ cup of water, eggs and salt; knead well. Let stand to rest.

8 ounces sausage
½ cup chopped mushrooms
1 (3-pound) beef tenderloin
1 egg yolk, beaten
1 tablespoon water

Pastry
10 tablespoons butter
4 cups flour
½ cup water
2 eggs, beaten
Salt to taste

Yield: 8 to 10 servings

Tenderloin Stuffed with Lobster

$\mathcal{M}$ake this main course the centerpiece
for a sumptuous dinner.

1 (3- to 4-pound) beef
tenderloin
2 (4-ounce) frozen lobster
tails, cooked
1 tablespoon melted butter
1½ teaspoons lemon juice
6 slices bacon, partially
cooked

Aioli Sauce
3 garlic cloves, minced
1 tablespoon kosher salt
3 egg yolks
2 cups olive oil

Yield: 8 servings

Preheat the oven to 425 degrees.

Butterfly the beef tenderloin. Remove the lobster meat from the shells. Slice the lobster meat into halves lengthwise. Arrange the lobster meat end to end over the cut side of the tenderloin. Drizzle with a mixture of melted butter and lemon juice.

Roll the tenderloin lengthwise to enclose the lobster. Tie with kitchen twine at 1-inch intervals. Place the tenderloin on a rack in a baking pan.

Bake at 450 degrees for 5 to 6 minutes per pound for rare or until meat thermometer registers 120 to 125 degrees. Arrange the bacon on top. Bake for 5 minutes longer. Remove to a warm serving platter.

Serve Aioli Sauce with the beef tenderloin.

Aioli Sauce

Crush the garlic using the flat side of a chef's knife and mix with salt in a bowl until a paste forms. Whisk in the egg yolks.

Add the olive oil a few drops at a time, whisking constantly until thick. Whisk in a few drops of warm water to prevent the emulsion from breaking. Add the remaining olive oil in a fine stream and add a few drops of warm water, whisking constantly.

Note: Aioli Sauce is simply a mayonnaise made with garlic. Serve this versatile sauce with anything from seafood to red meat. It also is a wonderful dip for blanched vegetables.

Mustard Marinated Sirloin

This simply prepared mushroom sauce is also wonderful with chicken, pork or game. Be sure to marinate the sirloin ahead of time.

Combine the mustard, 2 tablespoons red wine, pepper and garlic in a bowl; mix well. Coat both sides of the steak with the mustard mixture. Place the steak in a shallow dish. Marinate, covered, in the refrigerator for 8 hours.

Preheat the broiler.

Place the steak on a greased rack in a broiler pan. Broil 4 inches from the heat source with the oven door partially open for 4 to 5 minutes per side or until done to taste. Let stand for 5 minutes. Slice across the grain.

Pour Mushroom Sauce over the steak.

Mushroom Sauce

Sauté the mushrooms in butter in a skillet over medium heat. Add the flour; mix well. Cook for 1 minute, stirring constantly. Add the broth and ½ cup red wine. Cook until thickened, stirring constantly. Season with the salt and pepper.

2 tablespoons Dijon mustard
2 tablespoons dry red wine
1 teaspoon coarsely ground
    pepper
2 cloves of garlic, minced
1 (1-pound) lean boneless
    sirloin steak, trimmed

Mushroom Sauce
1 cup sliced fresh mushrooms
2 tablespoons butter
1½ tablespoons flour
1 cup beef broth
½ cup dry red wine
¼ teaspoon salt
¼ teaspoon pepper

Yield: 2 to 3 servings

Veal Cutlets with Tomato Coulis

The tomato coulis is scrumptious. Serve this lovely veal dish with pasta and a simple green salad.

8 veal cutlets
Flour
Salt and pepper to taste
2 eggs, slightly beaten
1 cup (or more) fresh
bread crumbs
Grated Parmesan cheese
Zest of 2 lemons
1 to 2 tablespoons olive oil
1 to 2 tablespoons butter

Tomato Coulis
Thyme sprigs
Basil sprigs
Parsley sprigs
1 medium onion, minced
2 cloves of garlic, minced
2 cups peeled and seeded
Roma tomatoes
Salt and pepper to taste

Yield: 8 servings

Flatten the veal between sheets of waxed paper. Coat each slice with a mixture of flour, salt and pepper. Dip in the eggs; roll in a mixture of bread crumbs, cheese and lemon zest.

Sauté the veal in a mixture of olive oil and butter until light brown on both sides. Remove to a serving platter. Garnish with lemon wedges and sprigs of basil and thyme. Serve with the warm Tomato Coulis.

Tomato Coulis

Tie the thyme, basil and parsley sprigs together with kitchen twine.

Sauté the onion and garlic in a nonstick skillet coated with nonstick cooking spray. Add the herbs, tomatoes, salt and pepper; mix well. Simmer over low heat until the tomatoes are reduced slightly, stirring frequently; discard the herbs. Process the mixture in a food processor until smooth. Return to the skillet. Keep warm.

Veal Tenderloin Rolls

Veal stuffed with prosciutto and brie in a mushroom and cream sauce—so many wonderful flavors in one dish.

Pound the veal between sheets of waxed paper. Season with the salt and pepper. Spread each slice with a mixture of the prosciutto and brie cheese. Roll to enclose the filling; coat with the flour.

Sauté the veal rolls in the butter in a skillet over medium-high heat until cooked through and brown. Remove to a warm covered serving dish.

Sauté the mushrooms and shallots in the pan drippings. Stir in the cream and bring to a boil. Cook until sauce is of the desired consistency, stirring constantly. Stir in the parsley and lemon juice. Season with salt. Spoon over the veal rolls.

16 (1½-ounce) slices veal tenderloin
Salt and pepper to taste
2 thin slices prosciutto, finely chopped
8 ounces brie cheese, at room temperature
¼ cup flour
1 cup unsalted butter
4 ounces mushrooms, chopped
3 shallots, finely chopped
1 cup whipping cream
1 cup chopped fresh parsley
Fresh lemon juice

Yield: 6 to 8 servings

Grilled Pork Tenderloin

The slightly sweet marinade gives the tenderloin flavor and character. Leftovers make fabulous sandwiches.

3 tablespoons Dijon mustard

2 tablespoons olive oil

1 tablespoon cracked black pepper

1/2 teaspoon ground cardamom

2 tablespoons honey

2 tablespoons balsamic vinegar

1/2 teaspoon cinnamon

1/2 teaspoon ground ginger

1 (2- to 3-pound) trimmed pork tenderloin

4 sprigs of fresh rosemary

Yield: 6 to 8 servings

Combine the mustard, olive oil, pepper, cardamom, honey, vinegar, cinnamon and ginger in a bowl; mix well. Add the pork. Marinate, covered, in the refrigerator overnight.

Soak the rosemary in water to cover in a bowl for 10 minutes. Place on grill rack over medium-hot coals. Remove pork from marinade.

Grill the pork until cooked through, turning occasionally. Let pork stand for 15 minutes before slicing.

Roasted Pork Loin with Balsamic Glaze

*P*ork and fruit have always been a winning
combination. This fresh, innovative pork dish
is finished with grilled oranges and a succulent
orange balsamic glaze.

Pierce the pork roast in several places with a fork. Place in an oven-cooking bag or a 2-gallon sealable plastic bag.

Combine the orange juice concentrate, balsamic vinegar, olive oil, thyme, orange rind, garlic, salt, black pepper and red pepper in a bowl; mix well. Pour ½ cup of the marinade over the pork roast; reserve the remaining marinade. Marinate in the refrigerator for 4 hours or longer, turning occasionally.

Preheat the grill.

Combine the orange slices, water and reserved marinade in a bowl; mix well. Set aside.

Drain the pork, reserving the marinade. Place the pork on the grill rack 4 to 5 inches from the hot coals. Grill over medium-high coals for 1 to 1½ hours or until meat thermometer registers 160 degrees, basting with the reserved marinade during the first 30 minutes of grilling. Remove the pork to a serving platter; cover with foil.

Drain the liquid from the orange slices into a saucepan. Grill the orange slices over hot coals for 2 minutes per side. Arrange slices on the serving platter.

Cut the pork into ½-inch slices. Pour the accumulated meat juices into the saucepan; mix well. Bring just to a boil; drizzle over the pork. Garnish with thyme sprigs.

Flavor of the pork roast is enhanced with standing time before slicing and serving.

*1 (4½-pound) boneless pork
  loin roast, trimmed, tied*
*1 (6-ounce) can frozen orange
  juice concentrate, thawed*
½ cup balsamic vinegar
¼ cup olive oil
*2 tablespoons chopped fresh
  thyme or 2 teaspoons
  dried thyme*
*1 tablespoon grated orange
  rind*
*3 large cloves of garlic,
  minced*
1 teaspoon salt
½ teaspoon black pepper
*¼ teaspoon crushed red
  pepper*
*4 peeled or unpeeled navel
  oranges, cut into ½-inch
  slices*
¼ cup water

Yield: 10 to 12 servings

Pork Schnitzel with Sour Cream Dill Sauce

Schnitzel is traditionally made with veal, but pork is a delicious and inexpensive alternative. Garnish with thinly sliced lemons.

1 pound pork tenderloin, cut into 6 slices

⅓ cup flour

1 teaspoon seasoned salt or salt

¼ teaspoon pepper

1 egg, beaten

2½ tablespoons milk

¾ cup fine dried bread crumbs

1 teaspoon paprika

3 tablespoons shortening

Sour Cream Dill Sauce

¾ cup chicken broth

1 tablespoon flour

¼ teaspoon dried dill

½ cup sour cream

Yield: 6 servings

Pound the pork ⅛ to ¼ inch thick between sheets of waxed paper; cut small slits around edge to prevent curling.

Coat the pork in a mixture of flour, seasoned salt and pepper; dip in a mixture of egg and milk. Roll in a mixture of the bread crumbs and paprika.

Cook 3 cutlets at a time in the shortening in a skillet for 2 to 3 minutes per side or until cooked through; drain, reserving the skillet drippings. Remove the cutlets to a serving platter; keep warm. Garnish with lemon slices and sprigs of fresh dill. Serve with Sour Cream Dill Sauce.

Sour Cream Dill Sauce

Stir the broth into the reserved drippings in the skillet, scraping to loosen the brown particles. Stir in a mixture of flour, dill and sour cream. Cook over low heat until thickened, stirring constantly. Cook for 1 to 2 minutes longer or until of the desired consistency, stirring constantly.

Down Home Chili

A terrific chili recipe—a home run every time.

Combine the tomatoes, celery, onion, green pepper, brown sugar, green chiles, broth, beer, chili powder, salt, garlic, oregano, cumin, pepper, thyme and coriander in a stockpot; mix well.

Cut the pork chops and steak into bite-sized pieces. Brown the pork in the oil in a skillet; drain. Stir into the tomato mixture. Brown the steak in the pan drippings in the skillet; drain. Stir into the tomato mixture.

Simmer, covered, for 2 to 3 hours or until of the desired consistency, stirring occasionally. Stir in the Monterey Jack cheese and lime juice just before serving. Ladle into chili bowls. Serve with tortilla chips.

Prepare 1 day in advance to enhance the flavor.

3½ cups stewed plum tomatoes, seeded, chopped
2 tablespoons finely chopped celery
2 cups coarsely chopped onion
¾ cup coarsely chopped green bell pepper
2 teaspoons brown sugar
3 long green chiles, roasted, peeled, chopped
1 (14-ounce) can beef broth
1 (12-ounce) can beer
2½ tablespoons chili powder
2 teaspoons salt
2 cloves of garlic, minced
1½ teaspoons each oregano, ground cumin and pepper
½ teaspoon each thyme and minced fresh coriander
2½ pounds pork chops
2 pounds flank or round steak
2 to 4 tablespoons vegetable oil
8 ounces shredded Monterey Jack cheese
3 tablespoons fresh lime juice

Yield: 8 to 10 servings

Sausage and Nut Strudel

This is a delicious and different choice for a brunch. Working with phyllo is easier than you might think. Remember to keep the phyllo from drying out.

1½ pounds link sausage, cooked, drained, cut into thin slices

12 ounces cream cheese, softened

½ cup sliced almonds

½ cup coarsely chopped pecans

½ cup coarsely chopped walnuts

1 large shallot, minced

1 teaspoon crushed dried thyme

1 teaspoon salt

9 sheets phyllo pastry

½ cup melted butter

Fine dried bread crumbs

Yield: 9 servings

Preheat the oven to 400 degrees. Combine the sausage, cream cheese, almonds, pecans, walnuts, shallot, thyme and salt in a bowl; mix well. Divide into 18 portions (about ⅓ cup each). Shape into 18 logs.

Place 1 sheet of the phyllo dough on a work surface with the long edge nearest you; cover remaining phyllo dough with plastic wrap to keep moist.

Brush the right half of the sheet of the phyllo dough with the melted butter; sprinkle with the bread crumbs. Fold the left side over to cover. Brush the bottom half of the folded phyllo dough with the melted butter; sprinkle with the bread crumbs. Fold the top half over to cover. Brush the entire surface with the melted butter; cut into halves horizontally. Place 1 sausage log vertically on 1 of the phyllo dough halves; fold long ends over to cover log. Roll phyllo dough from short end to enclose filling. Brush with melted butter. Arrange in a baking pan. Repeat the process with the remaining phyllo dough and sausage logs.

Bake at 400 degrees for 30 to 35 minutes or until light golden brown. Remove to a serving platter. Garnish with cherry tomatoes. Serve hot or warm.

Honey Mustard Pecan Roasted Lamb

Spectacular for a special event or a Sunday dinner.

Process the pecans, bread crumbs and rosemary in a food processor until well mixed.

Brown 1 rack of lamb in the olive oil in a skillet over high heat, turning every 5 minutes; pat dry. Transfer to a roasting pan. Repeat the process with the remaining rack of lamb. Spread both sides of the lamb with a mixture of the Dijon mustard, honey, molasses and garlic.

Preheat the oven to 375 degrees.

Arrange the lamb rounded side up; sprinkle with the pecan mixture. Roast at 375 degrees for 25 minutes or until meat thermometer registers 130 to 135 degrees for medium-rare. Cut between the ribs to separate into chops.

½ cup toasted pecans
3 tablespoons fresh bread
   crumbs
1 teaspoon minced fresh
   rosemary or ¼ teaspoon
   dried rosemary
2 (1¼-pound) racks of lamb,
   trimmed
2 tablespoons olive oil
¼ cup Dijon mustard
1 tablespoon honey
1 tablespoon light molasses
2 small cloves of garlic,
   minced

Yield: 6 to 8 servings

Roasted Rack of Lamb with

Chef Michael Turner of The Green Bottle Grill in Huntsville contributes this outstanding lamb recipe.

1 rack of lamb, split, with
chine bone removed
Minced garlic to taste
Rosemary to taste
Thyme to taste
Minced fresh parsley to taste
Olive oil to taste
Salt and pepper to taste
Chopped shallots
Red wine
Minced fresh herbs to taste
Butter to taste

Arrange the lamb in a shallow dish. Combine garlic, rosemary, thyme and parsley with enough olive oil to coat in a bowl; mix well. Pour over the lamb, turning to coat.

Marinate, covered, in the refrigerator for 8 to 10 hours, turning occasionally. Remove the lamb from the marinade; pat dry. Sprinkle with salt and pepper.

Preheat the oven to 450 degrees.

Sear the lamb in a skillet coated with olive oil. Transfer to a heavy baking pan. Bake at 450 degrees until done to taste. Remove the lamb to a warm platter. Cut into chops.

Stir the shallots, red wine and fresh herbs into the pan drippings. Cook until of the desired consistency, stirring constantly. Season with salt, pepper, butter and parsley to taste.

Spoon the Caponata in the center of each dinner plate. Arrange the lamb chops around the Eggplant Caponata; drizzle with the wine sauce.

Fresh Eggplant Caponata

Eggplant Caponata

Preheat the oven to 350 degrees. Coat the eggplant and zucchini with the vegetable oil. Arrange in a baking pan.

Bake at 350 degrees for 15 minutes.

Sauté the onion in the olive oil in a skillet until tender. Stir in the celery and garlic. Cook for 2 to 3 minutes or until tender, stirring frequently. Add the tomatoes, olives, capers, pine nuts and raisins; mix well. Stir in the sugar, vinegar, salt and pepper.

Cook just until heated through, stirring constantly. Stir in the eggplant and zucchini.

Eggplant Caponata

1 eggplant, chopped
1 zucchini, chopped
1 to 2 tablespoons vegetable oil
1 red onion, chopped
1 to 2 tablespoons olive oil
1 stalk celery, chopped
3 cloves of garlic, minced
3 tomatoes, chopped
1/4 cup pitted olives
2 tablespoons capers
2 tablespoons toasted pine nuts
1/4 cup golden raisins
Sugar to taste
Vinegar to taste
Salt and freshly ground pepper
 to taste

Yield: 4 to 6 servings

Grilled Lamb Kabobs

*W*hen a summer evening calls for a sophisticated dinner al fresco, grill these stunning lamb kabobs.

2 pounds leg of lamb, cut into 1½-inch cubes
1 stalk fresh rosemary
4 yellow bell peppers
4 red bell peppers
2 red onions
1 pound fresh mushroom caps
16 cherry tomatoes
2 tablespoons extra-virgin olive oil
Salt and pepper to taste

Lamb Marinade
2 cloves of garlic
¼ cup fresh oregano
1 teaspoon pepper
1 cup red wine
⅓ cup wine vinegar
1 bay leaf
1 tablespoon honey
3 tablespoons extra-virgin olive oil

Yield: 4 servings

Skewer each cube of lamb with a 2-inch piece of the rosemary stalk. Combine the cubes and Lamb Marinade in a bowl turning to coat. Marinate for 1 hour or longer. Preheat the grill.

Slice the peppers and the onions into 1½-inch squares or triangles. Thread the lamb cubes alternately with the peppers, onions, mushroom caps and tomatoes onto skewers.

Brush the kabobs with olive oil; sprinkle with salt and pepper. Grill the lamb, turning the kabobs one quarter turn every few minutes, basting with the Lamb Marinade.

The kabobs may be served on a bed of rice pilaf or couscous.

Lamb Marinade

Combine the garlic, oregano, pepper, wine, wine vinegar, bay leaf, honey and olive oil in a large bowl; whisk gently until well blended.

Madison County Barbecued Dove

Have this spicy barbeque sauce on hand for grilling to celebrate the opening day of dove season.

Preheat the grill. Rinse the dove and pat dry. Place 1 onion quarter and 1 jalapeño quarter in each dove cavity; wrap with the bacon.

Combine the butter, vinegar, Worcestershire sauce, sugar, garlic, prepared mustard, catsup, lemon juice, water and Tabasco sauce in a saucepan; mix well.

Simmer for 20 minutes, stirring occasionally. Brush the dove with the sauce.

Grill the dove over medium-high coals for 10 minutes or until cooked through. Remove to a serving platter; drizzle with barbecue sauce.

Note: Use this barbecue sauce when grilling any type of meat or poultry, but remember any barbecue sauce that contains sugar will caramelize if cooked for more than 15 minutes, particularly if used when grilling.

8 dove breasts

2 onions, cut into quarters

2 jalapeños, seeded, cut into quarters

8 slices bacon

1/2 cup butter

1/4 cup vinegar

1/4 cup Worcestershire sauce

1/4 cup sugar or 1/2 cup honey

1 clove of garlic, crushed

1 tablespoon prepared mustard

2 cups catsup

1/4 cup lemon juice

1/2 cup water

2 tablespoons Tabasco sauce

Yield: 4 servings

Roast Duck with Orange Glaze

A classic preparation. Orange Glaze is just right with the assertive, rich flavor of duck. Wild rice and broccoli are easy accompaniments to any game.

1 (4- to 5-pound) duck
1 to 2 apples, cut into quarters
1 large onion, cut into quarters

Orange Glaze
⅓ cup packed brown sugar
1 tablespoon (or more) cornstarch
⅓ cup sugar
1 cup orange juice
1 tablespoon grated orange rind
¼ teaspoon salt

Yield: 4 to 6 servings

Preheat the oven to 325 degrees. Rinse the duck inside and out; pat dry. Place the apples and onion inside the duck cavity. Arrange the duck in a roasting pan.

Roast at 325 degrees for 40 minutes per pound; discard the apples and onion. Remove to a serving platter; keep warm.

Drizzle some of the Orange Glaze over the duck. Serve the remaining Orange Glaze with the duck.

Orange Glaze

Combine the brown sugar, cornstarch and sugar in a saucepan; mix well. Stir in the orange juice, orange rind and salt.

Cook over low heat until the sugar dissolves, stirring constantly; reduce heat. Simmer for 3 minutes or until thickened, stirring constantly.

Grilled Quail with Black-Eyed Pea Salad

Quail are tender and have a lovely, mild flavor featured in this simple, supremely Southern recipe.

Rinse the quail inside and out; pat dry. Arrange in a shallow dish. Combine the garlic, onion, thyme, rosemary and parsley with enough olive oil to coat in a bowl; mix well. Pour over the quail, tossing to coat.

Marinate, covered, in the refrigerator for 24 hours, turning occasionally. Drain the quail. Season with salt and pepper.

Preheat the grill. Grill over hot coals for 3 to 4 minutes per side or until cooked through. Let stand for several minutes; split the quail.

Arrange the quail on warm dinner plates; spoon the Black-Eyed Pea Salad on the plate. Drizzle with additional olive oil. Garnish with fresh herbs.

Black-Eyed Pea Salad

Combine the black-eyed peas, bell peppers, tomatoes, red onion, wine vinegar, olive oil, parsley, shallots, salt and pepper in a stainless steel bowl; mix well.

Chill, covered, for 3 hours. Let stand at room temperature for 1 hour before serving.

8 semi-boneless quail

10 cloves of garlic, lightly crushed

1 onion, sliced

2 sprigs each of thyme, rosemary and parsley

Olive oil

Salt and pepper to taste

Black-Eyed Pea Salad

4 cups rinsed cooked black-eyed peas, chilled

1 red bell pepper, chopped

1 yellow bell pepper, chopped

3 tomatoes, peeled, seeded, chopped

1 red onion, chopped

1/4 cup white wine vinegar

1/2 cup extra-virgin olive oil

1/4 cup chopped fresh parsley

2 tablespoons chopped shallots

Salt and pepper to taste

Yield: 4 servings

Grilled Venison Tenderloin

If you are lucky enough to have a hunter in the family to bring home this most desirable cut of meat, try this outstanding recipe.

1 to 2 venison tenderloins
1 cup vinegar
½ cup Dale's steak seasoning
¼ cup red wine
½ cup melted butter or margarine

Yield: 8 to 10 servings

Arrange the tenderloins in a deep dish. Pour the vinegar over the tenderloins. Add enough water to cover completely. Marinate, covered, in the refrigerator for 3 hours; drain. Rinse with cold water; drain.

Place the tenderloins in a covered container. Pour a mixture of the steak seasoning, red wine and butter over the tenderloins, tossing to coat.

Marinate the tenderloins in the refrigerator for 3 hours or longer, turning occasionally.

Preheat the grill. Grill over medium hot coals for 8 minutes per side or until done to taste.

Pan-Roasted Rabbit with Linguini

Tender and versatile, rabbit adapts well to almost any recipe in which chicken is the usual choice.

Preheat the oven to 450 degrees. Cook the linguini in boiling salted water using package directions; drain. Rinse with cold water; drain.

Season the rabbit with salt and pepper; coat lightly with flour. Sear the rabbit legs in the olive oil in a sauté pan. Remove to a baking pan.

Bake at 450 degrees for 5 minutes. Add the loins to the baking pan. Bake until the legs are cooked through and the loins are medium-rare. Remove the rabbit to a platter.

Stir the shallots into the pan drippings. Add the white wine. Stir to deglaze the pan. Cook until the liquid is reduced. Stir in the stock. Cook over medium-high heat until the liquid is reduced, stirring constantly. Stir in the Dijon mustard and thyme. Add the butter, salt and pepper. Cook just until heated through.

Reheat the linguini. Toss with the parsley, olive oil, salt and pepper in a bowl. Arrange the pasta on warm dinner plates. Place the rabbit legs on the pasta; top with the wine sauce. Slice the loin; arrange around the rabbit legs. Sprinkle with the bacon.

12 ounces linguini
Salt to taste
4 rabbit hind legs
4 rabbit loins
Pepper to taste
Flour
Olive oil
1 tablespoon chopped shallots
¼ cup white wine
1 cup chicken stock
2 tablespoons Dijon mustard
Thyme to taste
1 tablespoon butter
½ cup chopped fresh parsley
3 ounces crisp-fried bacon, crumbled

Yield: 4 servings

Chicken Breasts with Curry Chutney Butter

These exotic chicken packets take advantage of the great flavor of chutney. This recipe can be assembled ahead of time and is easily doubled.

4 teaspoons butter
4 boneless, skinless chicken breast halves
1 cup thinly sliced carrots
1 cup thinly sliced zucchini
4 teaspoons cold water
½ teaspoon salt
¼ teaspoon pepper
½ cup mango chutney
2 tablespoons melted butter
1 tablespoon curry powder
¼ cup chopped unsalted peanuts
1 to 4 tablespoons flaked coconut

Yield: 4 servings

Preheat the oven to 500 degrees. Cut four 12x14-inch sheets of foil. Spread 1 teaspoon of the butter in the center of the lower half of each sheet. Rinse the chicken and pat dry.

For each packet, place one-fourth of the carrot and one-fourth of the zucchini slices on the buttered portion of each sheet of the foil. Sprinkle with the water; top with the chicken. Sprinkle with the salt and pepper. Mix the chutney, 2 tablespoons melted butter and curry powder and divide among the four packets. Sprinkle each with peanuts and coconut. Seal foil tightly. Place packets seam side up on a baking sheet.

Bake at 500 degrees for 15 to 20 minutes or until the chicken is cooked through and the vegetables are tender.

Buttermilk Pecan Chicken

A nutty coating makes this chicken special.
Note the Parslied Rice to serve with other dishes as well.

Preheat the oven to 350 degrees. Rinse the chicken and pat dry. Melt the butter in a 9x13-inch baking pan.

Combine the flour, ground pecans, sesame seeds, paprika, salt and pepper in a bowl; mix well.

Dip the chicken into a mixture of the egg and buttermilk; coat with the flour mixture. Arrange in the prepared baking pan, turning once to coat with the butter.

Bake at 350 degrees for 30 minutes or until cooked through. Sprinkle with the chopped pecans 5 minutes before the end of the baking time. Serve with Parslied Rice.

Parslied Rice

Sauté the onion and garlic in the oil in a large saucepan until tender. Add the water, rice, bouillon cubes and lemon juice; mix well. Bring to a boil; reduce heat.

Simmer, covered, for 20 minutes or until the rice is tender and the liquid has been absorbed. Stir in the parsley.

8 boneless skinless chicken
    breast halves
1/3 cup butter or margarine
1 cup flour
1 cup ground pecans
1/4 cup sesame seeds
1 tablespoon paprika
1 1/2 teaspoons salt
1/8 teaspoon pepper
1 egg, lightly beaten
1 cup buttermilk
1/4 cup chopped pecans

Parslied Rice
1 medium onion, chopped
2 cloves of garlic, minced
1 tablespoon vegetable oil
4 cups water
2 cups uncooked long grain
    rice
4 chicken bouillon cubes
3 tablespoons lemon juice
1/2 cup chopped fresh parsley

Yield: 8 servings

Grilled Balsamic Chicken Breasts

*F*resh herbs and balsamic vinegar take chicken breasts from ordinary to extraordinary. Garnish with additional fresh herbs and serve hot or cold.

2 to 4 boneless chicken
breast halves
¼ cup balsamic vinegar
2 shallots, chopped
2 cloves of garlic, chopped
2 tablespoons chopped
fresh thyme
Salt and pepper to taste

Vinaigrette
1 cup homemade
chicken stock
½ cup dry white wine
⅓ cup balsamic vinegar
2 tablespoons chopped fresh
thyme or rosemary
2 tablespoons chopped
fresh Italian parsley
¼ cup golden raisins

Yield: 2 to 4 servings

Rinse the chicken and pat dry. Pound ¾ inch thick between sheets of waxed paper. Place in a shallow dish.

Mix the balsamic vinegar, shallots, garlic, thyme, salt and pepper in a bowl. Pour over the chicken.

Marinate, covered, in the refrigerator for 2 hours or longer, turning occasionally. Let stand at room temperature for 30 minutes. Drain the chicken.

Preheat the grill. Grill over hot coals for 15 minutes or until cooked through, turning every 5 minutes. Remove to a serving platter. Serve with the Vinaigrette.

Vinaigrette

Combine the chicken stock and white wine in a saucepan; mix well. Cook until the liquid is reduced by one half, stirring frequently. Stir in the balsamic vinegar, thyme, parsley and golden raisins.

Simmer over low heat for 20 minutes, stirring occasionally.

Artichoke Chicken with Dijon Velouté Sauce

*A*rtichokes and sun-dried tomatoes add terrific
flavor to the rich filling in these rolled chicken breasts.

Artichoke Chicken

Preheat the oven to 350 degrees. Rinse the chicken and
pat dry. Pound until very thin and 1½ times original size between
plastic wrap.

Sauté the onion in the butter in a skillet. Add the cream
cheese. Cook until melted, stirring constantly. Remove from heat.
Add the artichokes, sun-dried tomatoes, bread crumbs, egg, salt,
black pepper and cayenne pepper; mix well. Let stand until cool.

Spoon about ¼ cup of the cream cheese mixture on the
edge of each chicken breast. Roll to enclose the filling. Arrange in
a greased baking pan.

Bake at 350 degrees for 30 minutes. Cool slightly. Cut into
1-inch slices.

Spoon the Dijon Velouté Sauce onto 6 dinner plates. Arrange
the chicken slices around the edge. Serve with your favorite rice.
Garnish with fresh herbs.

Dijon Velouté Sauce

Combine the honey mustard with the chicken stock in a
saucepan; mix well. Stir in the whipping cream. Whisk in a mixture
of the cornstarch and water.

Cook over medium heat until thickened, stirring constantly.

Artichoke Chicken

6 (8-ounce) whole boneless
   skinless chicken breasts
3 tablespoons finely chopped
   onion
3 tablespoons butter
4 ounces cream cheese
1 (16-ounce) can artichoke
   hearts, drained, chopped
9 oil-pack sun-dried tomatoes,
   chopped
½ cup bread crumbs
1 egg, beaten
Salt, black pepper and
   cayenne pepper to taste

Dijon Velouté Sauce
½ to 1 jar honey mustard
2 cups chicken stock
2 cups whipping cream
3 tablespoons cornstarch
¼ cup water

Yield: 6 servings

Peppered Chicken with Artichoke Purée

A pretty, flavorful main dish. Garnish with lime slices.

2 whole boneless chicken
breasts, split
2 egg whites, slightly beaten
2 tablespoons crushed black
peppercorns
Salt to taste
½ cup unsalted butter
2 teaspoons olive oil
2 teaspoons minced shallots
1 (9-ounce) package frozen
artichoke hearts, thawed
½ cup chicken broth
⅓ cup dry white wine
2 teaspoons fresh lime juice
½ teaspoon grated lime rind
⅓ cup whipping cream
Freshly ground pepper to taste

Yield: 4 servings

Rinse the chicken and pat dry. Dip in the egg whites; sprinkle with the peppercorns and salt.

Melt 2 tablespoons of the butter with the olive oil in a skillet over high heat. Add the chicken. Sauté for 3 to 5 minutes on each side or until cooked through. Remove to a warm platter.

Wipe the skillet clean. Sauté the shallots in 2 tablespoons of the butter in the skillet for 2 minutes. Stir in the artichokes, broth and white wine. Increase the heat to high.

Cook for 2 minutes or until the artichokes are heated through, stirring frequently. Process the mixture in a food processor until puréed. Return the purée to the skillet. Stir in the lime juice, lime rind, whipping cream and remaining ¼ cup butter. Cook until the butter melts and the purée is heated through, stirring constantly. Season with the freshly ground pepper and salt.

Spoon the purée onto 4 dinner plates; top with the chicken.

Lime Marinated Chicken Breasts

Cook extra to use for sandwiches or in green salads.

Rinse the chicken and pat dry. Arrange in a shallow dish. Mix the soy sauce, lime juice, Worcestershire sauce, garlic, dry mustard and pepper in a bowl. Pour over the chicken, turning to coat with the marinade. Marinate, covered, in the refrigerator for 30 minutes.

Heat a nonstick skillet sprayed with butter-flavor nonstick cooking spray. Add the chicken. Cook over medium heat for 6 minutes on each side or until the chicken is cooked through.

4 boneless skinless chicken breast halves
½ cup soy sauce
¼ cup lime juice
1 tablespoon Worcestershire sauce
2 cloves of garlic, crushed
½ teaspoon each dry mustard and ground pepper

Yield: 4 servings

French Garlic Chicken

Slow cooking mellows the garlic.

Preheat the oven to 350 degrees. Soak garlic in boiling water in a bowl for 3 minutes or until skins are loosened. Drain and trim garlic, discarding skins.

Rinse the chicken and pat dry. Sprinkle with the seasonings. Add the garlic. Tie the wings and legs; rub with a small amount of corn oil. Place in a heavy 4-quart baking pan.

Bake, tightly covered, at 350 degrees for 1½ hours or until the chicken is cooked through and the garlic is tender.

20 cloves of garlic
1 (3- to 4-pound) chicken
Salt and pepper to taste
6 (3-inch) sprigs of rosemary
¼ teaspoon tarragon

Yield: 4 servings

Chicken Breasts Niçoise

Summer grilling becomes a special event with this mouth-watering main dish.

6 small boneless skinless
chicken breast halves
½ teaspoon minced
fresh thyme
Freshly ground pepper to taste
2 tablespoons fresh
lemon juice
1 tablespoon extra-virgin
olive oil
½ cup chopped niçoise olives
¼ cup minced green onions
1 small clove of garlic, minced
2 teaspoons capers
¼ to ½ teaspoon fresh
lemon juice
¼ teaspoon tomato paste
12 thin slices bacon
6 bay leaves
6 sprigs of thyme

Yield: 6 servings

Rinse the chicken and pat dry. Arrange in a dish. Sprinkle both sides with the thyme and pepper; drizzle with 2 tablespoons lemon juice and olive oil.

Marinate, covered, for 8 hours, turning occasionally.

Combine the olives, green onions, garlic, capers, ¼ teaspoon lemon juice and tomato paste in a bowl; mix well. Taste and add the remaining ¼ teaspoon lemon juice if desired.

Blanch the bacon in boiling water in a skillet for 5 minutes; drain. Rinse with water and pat dry.

Preheat the grill.

Drain the chicken. Pound ¼ inch thick between sheets of waxed paper. Spoon 2 rounded teaspoons of the olive mixture in the center of each chicken breast. Fold 1 side over to enclose the filling; fold in both ends and roll. Wrap 2 bacon slices around each roll; secure with wooden picks. Place 1 bay leaf under the bacon on 1 side and 1 sprig of the thyme under the bacon on the other side.

Grill the chicken for 10 minutes on each side or until the bacon is crisp and the chicken is cooked through. Discard the wooden picks and bay leaves. Cut across the grain into thin slices. Serve immediately.

Grilled Cornish Hens

A delightful change of pace. Wild rice is a perfect accompaniment.

Preheat the grill. Rake the whitened coals to one end of the grill.

Remove the giblets from the hens. Rinse the hens with cold water and pat dry.

Rinse the shallots and pat dry. Place a shallot in the cavity of each hen. Sprinkle hens with the Greek seasoning and rosemary.

Combine the butter, hot pepper sauce and Worcestershire sauce in a small bowl. Brush some of the mixture over the hens.

Place the hens at the opposite end of the grill from the coals. Grill, covered, for 1¼ hours or until tender, basting occasionally with the remaining butter mixture.

2 Cornish hens
2 shallots
1 teaspoon Greek seasoning
1 teaspoon dried whole
   rosemary, crushed
½ cup melted butter
¼ teaspoon hot pepper sauce
¼ teaspoon Worcestershire
   sauce

Yield: 2 servings

Heritage Fried Chicken

$\mathcal{N}$o single dish is as strongly identified with the South as fried chicken and no Alabama cookbook would be complete without this classic recipe. We are proud to offer this version from our own **Huntsville Heritage Cookbook**.

8 whole boneless chicken breasts
2 cups buttermilk
2 cups (about) self-rising flour
Seasoned salt,
salt and pepper to taste
Vegetable oil for frying

Yield: 8 servings

Soak the chicken in the buttermilk in an airtight container overnight; drain. Combine the flour, seasoned salt, salt and pepper in a covered container; mix well. Add the chicken; cover. Shake until the chicken is coated.

Preheat the oil to medium-hot in a skillet. Add the chicken. Fry until the chicken is tender and golden brown.

Note: Discard and replenish the oil if the sediment begins to burn while frying.

The Deep South is at its best in early May, when the last cold spell is over and the heat has not yet arrived. Leaves and grass are still the tender green of Easter. Wild flowers liven the countryside and, above all, the magnolia starts to bloom. Days grow long and fireflies light up the slow-falling darkness.

Mary Ward Brown
Fruit of the Season

Lobster with Tomato Saffron Sauce

*P**ull out all the stops with this superb lobster lunch or dinner.***

Spoon Tomato Saffron Sauce onto individual serving plates. Slice the cooked lobster tail meat into rounds and arrange the slices on sauce. Add the lobster claw pieces. Top with the cucumber slices and fresh dill or cilantro.

Tomato Saffron Sauce

Melt the butter in a skillet over medium heat. Add the shallots. Sauté for 5 to 7 minutes or until the shallots are translucent and slightly browned. Add the tarragon, white pepper, fish stock, saffron and wine; mix well.

Bring to a boil and cook until reduced to about ½ cup. Stir in the tomato paste. Strain the sauce through a sieve into a bowl.

Add the mayonnaise, lemon juice, salt, black pepper and Tabasco sauce to the tomato mixture; mix well.

1 pound cooked lobster
1 cucumber, thinly sliced
Fresh dill or cilantro

Tomato Saffron Sauce
1 tablespoon butter
2 shallots, finely chopped
2 teaspoons chopped fresh
   tarragon
⅛ teaspoon white pepper
¾ cup fish stock or clam juice
Dash of powdered saffron
¾ cup white wine
1½ tablespoons tomato paste
½ cup mayonnaise
¾ teaspoon lemon juice
Salt and black pepper to taste
Dash of Tabasco sauce

Yield: 4 to 6 servings

Scampi Alexander with Lemon Rice

This appealing shrimp dish is simple enough to prepare anytime for your family; elegant enough for special guests. Easily doubled or tripled for a buffet dinner.

2 pounds large uncooked shrimp
½ cup melted butter
½ cup white wine
2 tablespoons amaretto
2 large cloves of garlic, minced
½ teaspoon salt
¼ teaspoon white pepper
Juice of 1 lemon
2 tablespoons chopped parsley
¼ cup sliced almonds
Parmesan cheese to taste

Lemon Rice
1 package long grain and wild rice mix
Grated rind of 2 lemons

Yield: 4 servings

Peel the shrimp, leaving the tails attached. Place in a shallow baking dish.

Combine the butter, wine, amaretto, garlic, salt, pepper, lemon juice, parsley and almonds in a small bowl; mix well. Pour the marinade over the shrimp. Let stand, covered, at room temperature for 1 hour.

Preheat the oven to 500 degrees. Bake, uncovered, at 500 degrees for 10 to 12 minutes or just until the shrimp turn pink. Remove from the oven; sprinkle with Parmesan cheese. Serve over Lemon Rice.

Lemon Rice

Prepare the rice according to package instructions. Stir the grated lemon rind into the cooked rice.

Shrimp and Cheese Grits

*W*e're glad that grits are back! Southerners have always known that grits are a wonderful foil for spicy foods.

Peel and devein the shrimp; rinse and pat dry.

Cook the bacon in a large skillet until crisp; remove bacon to paper towels to drain. Drain the skillet.

Heat a small amount of olive oil in the skillet. Add the shrimp. Sauté until the shrimp just begin to turn pink. Add the mushrooms, scallions and garlic. Sauté until the shrimp turn pink. Stir in the bacon, lemon juice, hot sauce, parsley, salt and pepper.

Spoon the Cheese Grits onto 4 warm individual serving plates. Spoon the shrimp mixture over the grits. Serve immediately.

Cheese Grits

Bring the water to a boil in a saucepan. Stir in the grits gradually; reduce the heat. Cook for 20 minutes or until thickened, stirring constantly. Stir in the salt and margarine.

Combine the grits, Cheddar cheese, Parmesan cheese, white pepper, cayenne pepper and nutmeg in a bowl; mix well.

1½ pounds fresh shrimp
6 slices bacon, chopped
Olive oil for sautéing
2 cups sliced fresh mushrooms
1¼ cups sliced scallions or green onions
1 or 2 large garlic cloves, minced
4 teaspoons lemon juice
Hot sauce to taste
Chopped fresh parsley to taste
Salt and pepper to taste

Cheese Grits
4 cups water
1 cup grits
½ teaspoon salt
¼ cup margarine
1 cup sharp Cheddar cheese
½ cup grated Parmesan cheese
White pepper, cayenne pepper and nutmeg to taste

Yield: 4 servings

Shrimp Marengo

A tantalizing combination of shrimp, bacon and mushrooms in a traditional tomato sauce.

3½ pounds shrimp

7 slices bacon

1 medium onion, chopped

1 clove of garlic, crushed

1 pound fresh mushrooms, sliced

1½ teaspoons oregano

1 tablespoon sugar

⅛ teaspoon pepper

1½ teaspoons basil

1 teaspoon salt

⅛ teaspoon hot pepper sauce

1 (28-ounce) can chopped tomatoes

1 (6-ounce) can tomato paste

1 (10-ounce) can beef consommé

4 to 5 teaspoons prepared mustard

¼ cup flour

½ cup water

Cooked rice

Yield: 8 to 10 servings

Cook the shrimp in boiling water in a large stockpot; drain well. Peel and devein the shrimp; place in a medium bowl and set aside.

Cut the bacon into small pieces. Cook in a skillet until crisp; remove to paper towels to drain.

Sauté the onion, garlic and mushrooms in the bacon drippings in the skillet until tender.

Add the oregano, sugar, pepper, basil, salt, hot pepper sauce, tomatoes, tomato paste, consommé, mustard, shrimp and crumbled bacon; mix well. Cook for 10 minutes, stirring frequently.

Whisk the flour and water in a small bowl until smooth. Stir into the shrimp mixture. Cook until thickened, stirring constantly.

Serve over hot cooked rice.

Red Snapper in Parchment

A neat meal in a package. Enjoy the herb-filled aroma as the packets are opened.

Preheat the oven to 500 degrees. Combine the butter, basil, tarragon, thyme, oregano and garlic in a small bowl; set aside.

Cut four 15-inch squares of baking parchment. Fold the pieces in half.

Combine the red pepper, snow peas, carrots, jicama and leeks in a medium bowl.

Unfold 1 parchment square and place 1 cup of the vegetable mixture on half the square. Place a fillet on top of the vegetables. Top with 1 tablespoon of the butter mixture.

Brush the edges of the parchment lightly with olive oil. Fold the parchment over and press the edges to seal. Fold the edges tightly to within 1 inch of the filling. Repeat with the remaining parchment, vegetables and snapper fillets.

Brush 2 baking sheets lightly with olive oil; place 2 parchment packets on each baking sheet.

Bake at 500 degrees for 6 minutes. Place each packet on an individual serving plate; cut a small cross on the top to allow the aroma and steam to escape.

Serve immediately.

Note: Substitute any mild, firm fish fillets.

¼ cup butter, softened
¼ teaspoon dried basil
¼ teaspoon dried tarragon
Pinch of dried thyme
Pinch of dried oregano
1 clove of garlic, minced
1 red bell pepper, julienned
1 cup snow peas
1 cup julienned carrots
½ cup julienned jicama
½ cup julienned leeks
4 red snapper fillets,
*   1½ inches thick*
Olive oil to taste

Yield: 4 servings

Paupiettes of Flounder with Shrimp

Gulf Coast flounder is a mild, tender fish that adapts well to this pleasing sauce.

¼ cup minced shallots
2 tablespoons unsalted butter
6 (4-ounce) flounder fillets
Salt and freshly ground white pepper to taste
12 medium to large shrimp, peeled, deveined
½ cup white wine or apple cider
1 cup whipping cream
2 teaspoons lemon juice

Yield: 3 to 6 servings

Preheat the oven to 425 degrees.

Sauté the shallots in unsalted butter in a small skillet until soft. Spread half the shallots in a lightly buttered 8-inch square baking dish.

Season the fillets with salt and white pepper. Sprinkle 1 teaspoon of the remaining shallots on the gray side of each fillet. Place 2 shrimp side by side and head to tail across each fillet.

Roll the fillet around the shrimp so that the shrimp tails stick out at each end. Place the fillets seam side down in the baking dish. Pour the wine or cider over the fish and cover with a sheet of buttered foil or waxed paper.

Bake at 425 degrees for 15 minutes or until the fish is nearly done and almost completely opaque. Turn off the oven. Pour the cooking liquid carefully into a large skillet. Return the fish, covered, to the oven.

Boil the cooking liquid in the skillet for about 6 minutes or until reduced to about 3 tablespoons syrupy liquid. Stir in the whipping cream and lemon juice. Cook over high heat for 3 minutes longer or until thickened, stirring constantly. Season the fillets with salt and white pepper.

Arrange on a warm serving platter or on individual plates. Cover with the sauce; serve immediately.

Fried Tennessee River Catfish

There's nothing quite like freshly caught catfish served with slaw, hush puppies and icy cold beer.

Preheat the oil in a deep fryer to 330 degrees. Cut the fillets into halves. Brush lightly with half the mustard.

Place the cornmeal, salt, black pepper and red pepper in a sealable plastic bag; seal and shake to mix. Drop the fillets into the bag 1 at a time and shake until coated. Remove each fillet; brush lightly with the remaining mustard. Return the fillet to the bag and shake again until coated.

Deep-fry the fillets until golden brown; drain well.

Vegetable oil for deep-frying
12 catfish fillets
1 cup prepared mustard
1¼ cups white cornmeal
Salt and black pepper to taste
1 teaspoon red pepper

Yield: 6 to 8 servings

Grilled Mahimahi with Mustard Glaze

Easy, delicious and low in fat.

Season the mahimahi lightly with salt and pepper. Place in a shallow dish. Mix the mustard, olive oil, lemon juice and oregano in a small bowl. Spread on both sides of the fish, reserving the remaining mixture. Chill, covered, for 30 minutes to 2 hours.

Preheat the grill. Spray a wire grilling basket with nonstick cooking spray. Place the mahimahi in the grilling basket. Grill for 3 to 5 minutes on each side, basting with the reserved mustard marinade. Garnish with fresh herbs.

1½ pounds mahimahi
Salt and ground pepper to taste
2 tablespoons Dijon mustard
1 tablespoon olive oil
1 teaspoon lemon juice
1 teaspoon chopped fresh
  oregano

Yield: 4 servings

Main Courses

Seafood Strudel with

From Chef Paul Seery of the Summit Club in Birmingham, Alabama. Assemble this scrumptious strudel in advance, then heat and serve.

7 sheets frozen phyllo dough
Melted butter
1 tablespoon chopped fresh chives
1 tablespoon chopped fresh dill

Seafood Mixture
¼ cup finely chopped mixed red and green bell peppers
¼ small onion, finely chopped
4 fresh mushrooms, thinly sliced
2 tablespoons vegetable oil
8 ounces fresh scallops
4 ounces fresh medium shrimp, peeled, deveined, cut into pieces
4 ounces lump crab meat
4 ounces sole, chopped

Prepare all mixtures before unwrapping phyllo, as it will dry out quickly. Then, place one sheet of phyllo on work surface; brush with melted butter. Place another sheet on top of buttered sheet. Repeat till all sheets are layered and buttered.

Reserve 2 tablespoons of the Cream Mixture.

Combine the Seafood Mixture with enough of the remaining Cream Mixture to moisten; do not make too moist. Add chives and dill; mix well.

Spoon onto phyllo dough; roll as tightly as possible to enclose filling. Place on a baking sheet; brush with butter. Chill for 30 minutes to overnight.

Preheat the oven to 400 degrees. Bake at 400 degrees for 20 to 25 minutes or until golden brown.

Slice strudel carefully. Place cut side up on individual serving plates. Drizzle with the Lemon Cream Sauce.

Seafood Mixture

Sauté the red and green peppers, onion and mushrooms in the oil in a medium saucepan over medium-high heat. Cook for 3 to 7 minutes, stirring occasionally.

Stir in the scallops, shrimp, crab meat and sole gradually. Cook for 8 to 10 minutes or until seafood is cooked through. Remove from heat. Drain, reserving 2 tablespoons liquid. Let the Seafood Mixture stand until cool.

Lemon Cream Sauce

Cream Mixture

Make a roux by melting the butter in a small saucepan and blending in the flour until a paste forms. Cook over low heat for 5 to 6 minutes, stirring frequently. Remove from heat; set aside.

Combine the cooking wine, shallot, clam juice and lemon juice in a medium saucepan. Cook until the mixture is reduced to ¼ cup.

Whisk in the cream. Bring to a light boil. Cook for 8 to 10 minutes or until the mixture is reduced, stirring constantly.

Whisk in the cooled roux. Cook for 2 to 3 minutes longer over low heat, whisking constantly. Pour into a shallow pan. Chill for 30 to 60 minutes.

Lemon Cream Sauce

Combine the reserved seafood liquid, Cream Mixture, lemon juice and cream in a small bowl. Whisk until smooth.

Cream Mixture
2 tablespoons butter
3 tablespoons flour
¼ cup dry white cooking wine
1 teaspoon minced shallot
2 tablespoons clam juice
2 tablespoons lemon juice
2 cups whipping cream

Lemon Cream Sauce
2 tablespoons reserved
    seafood liquid
2 tablespoons reserved
    Cream Mixture
Juice of 1 lemon
¼ cup whipping cream

Yield: 6 servings

Cajun Trout with Pecan Sauce

A yummy sauce of butter, whiskey and pecans poured over sautéed trout.

¼ *cup cornmeal*
¼ *cup flour*
1 *teaspoon thyme*
1 *teaspoon salt*
½ *teaspoon pepper*
½ *teaspoon cayenne pepper*
½ *teaspoon paprika*
4 *(4-ounce) rainbow trout fillets*
4 *tablespoons butter*
2 *tablespoons amaretto*
2 *tablespoons whiskey*
¼ *cup chopped pecans*

Yield: 2 to 4 servings

Combine the cornmeal, flour, thyme, salt, pepper, cayenne pepper and paprika in a sealable plastic bag, shaking to mix well. Place the fillets in the bag 1 at a time and shake to coat evenly.

Melt 2 tablespoons butter in a large skillet over medium-high heat. Add the fillets flesh side down. Cook for 2 minutes or until golden brown. Turn the fillets gently. Cook for 2 minutes longer. Remove the fillets to a serving platter.

Add the amaretto, whiskey, remaining 2 tablespoons butter and pecans to the skillet and mix well. Cook for 1 minute or until bubbly, stirring constantly.

Pour the sauce over the trout. Serve immediately.

Smoked Salmon Tart

delicate crust holds a succulent, rich seafood filling. The dough takes a bit of time to prepare, but the filling is a snap.

Pastry

Combine the all-purpose flour, cake flour, ¼ teaspoon salt and ¼ teaspoon pepper in a food processor. Add the butter; process until the mixture is crumbly. Sprinkle with the cold water gradually, processing until the mixture forms a ball; do not overprocess.

Wrap the dough in plastic wrap. Chill for 2 hours.

Roll the dough on a lightly floured surface. Fit into a greased 10-inch fluted tart pan with a removable bottom; trim the edge. Chill for 30 minutes.

Preheat the oven to 375 degrees. Place a foil collar over the top edge of the tart pastry. Bake at 375 degrees until light brown.

Salmon Filling

Layer the onions, leeks, salmon and scallions in the baked tart pastry. Beat eggs with the whipping cream, salt, pepper and nutmeg in a bowl. Pour over the layers.

Bake at 375 degrees for 20 to 25 minutes or until the custard sets.

Serve hot, cold or at room temperature.

Pastry
1½ cups all-purpose flour
½ cup cake flour
¼ teaspoon salt
¼ teaspoon freshly ground
   pepper
½ cup plus 2 tablespoons
   unsalted butter
6 to 8 tablespoons cold water

Salmon Filling
2 cups sliced onions
White portion of 2 sliced leeks
6 ounces smoked salmon,
   chopped
3 scallions, chopped
2 eggs, beaten
2 cups whipping cream
Salt and pepper to taste
Grated nutmeg to taste

Yield: 6 servings

Main Courses

Grilled Salmon with Avocado Citrus Salsa

The glorious colors in this Caribbean-inspired dish make a spectacular presentation. Serve with white basmati rice.

Avocado Citrus Salsa

Sections of 2 peeled oranges
2 small onions, chopped
2 cups chopped fresh pineapple
2 large tomatoes, peeled, seeded, chopped
½ cup olive oil
½ cup chopped fresh cilantro
6 small serranos or 2 (or more) jalapeños, chopped
1 avocado, chopped

Grilled Salmon

12 (6-ounce) center-cut salmon fillets with skin, 1½ inches thick
3 cups pink grapefruit juice
Fresh cilantro sprigs

Yield: 12 servings

Avocado Citrus Salsa

Cut the orange sections into halves and place in a medium bowl. Add the onions, pineapple, tomatoes, olive oil, cilantro and chiles; mix well.

Chill, covered, for up to 8 hours. Stir in the avocado just before serving.

Grilled Salmon

Place the salmon in a shallow dish. Pour the grapefruit juice over the salmon. Let stand at room temperature for 1 hour, turning occasionally.

Preheat the grill to medium-high. Place the salmon skin side down on the grill rack. Grill, covered, for 7 minutes or until the salmon flakes easily. Remove to a warm platter.

Spoon Avocado Citrus Salsa over the grilled salmon. Top with cilantro sprigs.

Note: For variation, add one 16-ounce can of black beans, drained and rinsed, to salsa.

IN MEMORY OF

Marble Dove with Meridian

Chip Cooper

*A sense of history and graceful patina of age characterize historic
Maple Hill Cemetery, founded around 1818. Amid the many
distinguished monuments to influential Alabamians is found the
Meridian Marker. This towering column commemorates the
Huntsville Meridian, which played a critical role in the division of
land in the Mississippi Territory in 1809.*

Photograph right:
In the kitchen of Alabama
Constitution Village.
Cream Biscuits
Whole Wheat Buttermilk Flapjacks
Old World Whole Wheat and
Walnut Loaves
Sweet Country Cornbread

Overleaf:
Italian Braided Bread with
Garlic and Herb Cheese
Tomato and Onion Salad
Fresh Mint Tea

Breads

꧁⚜꧂

*Imagine a morning
in late November. A coming of
winter morning more than twenty
years ago. Consider the kitchen
of a spreading old house in a
country town. A great black stove
is its main feature; but there is
also a big round table and a
fireplace with two rocking chairs
placed in front of it.
Just today the fireplace
commenced its seasonal roar.*

—Truman Capote
A Christmas Memory

Whole Wheat Buttermilk Flapjacks

When your family craves something extra-hearty, these easy flapjacks will hit the spot. They are a great way to start a day outdoors.

Preheat the griddle. Combine the flours, wheat germ, brown sugar, baking powder, baking soda and salt in a large bowl; mix well.

Beat the egg with buttermilk and oil. Stir the egg mixture into the flour mixture until well blended.

Pour the desired amount of batter onto a hot lightly oiled griddle. Bake until the flapjacks start to bubble and the bottoms are light brown; turn flapjacks over and bake until brown.

1 cup whole wheat flour
¼ cup all-purpose flour
2 tablespoons toasted
    wheat germ
1 tablespoon brown sugar
1 teaspoon baking powder
¼ teaspoon baking soda
½ teaspoon salt
1 egg, beaten
1¼ cups buttermilk
1 tablespoon vegetable oil

Yield: 8 flapjacks

Madison Dill Bread

This is a great-tasting white bread with just the right amount of dill. The cottage cheese makes it moist.

1 envelope dry yeast
¼ cup warm water
1 cup small curd cottage cheese
2 tablespoons sugar
1 tablespoon minced onion
1 teaspoon salt
2 teaspoons dill
1 egg
2 cups flour
¼ teaspoon baking soda
Melted butter

Yield: 2 small loaves

Dissolve the yeast in the warm water in a large bowl. Let stand for 10 minutes.

Add the cottage cheese, sugar, onion, salt, dill, egg, flour and baking soda; mix well.

Let rise, covered, for 1 hour. Punch the dough down and divide into 2 portions.

Shape each into a loaf; place in small greased loaf pans. Let rise, covered, until doubled in bulk.

Preheat the oven to 350 degrees. Bake at 350 degrees for 30 to 40 minutes or until golden brown. Brush tops with melted butter. Let cool before serving.

French Bread

This reliable recipe lends itself to a variety of bread shapes, including loaves and breadsticks or even a pizza crust.

Dissolve the yeast in hot water in a bowl. Add the sugar, salt and margarine. Stir in the flour. Knead on a lightly floured surface until smooth and elastic. Place in a greased bowl, turning to coat the surface. Let rise until doubled in bulk.

Shape into 2 loaves. Place on a baking sheet. Let rise until doubled in bulk.

Preheat the oven to 400 degrees.

Cut several diagonal slashes on the top of each loaf with a sharp knife. Bake at 400 degrees for 20 minutes or until golden brown.

Serve with Garlic Spread if desired.

Garlic Spread

Combine the butter, cheese, mayonnaise, garlic, parsley, oregano and basil in a medium bowl; mix well.

Cut loaves into halves lengthwise and spread with butter mixture; wrap in foil. Bake at 375 degrees for 20 minutes. Unwrap and broil for 5 minutes or until brown. Slice and serve warm.

2 envelopes dry yeast
2½ cups hot water
1 tablespoon sugar
1 tablespoon salt
2 tablespoons margarine
7 cups bread flour

Garlic Spread

1 cup butter, softened
1 cup freshly grated
    Parmesan cheese
½ cup mayonnaise
5 cloves of garlic, minced
3 tablespoons minced
    fresh parsley
½ teaspoon oregano
½ teaspoon basil

Yield: 2 loaves

Italian Braided Bread with

Savory and hearty, this braided bread is a delightful picnic food. Once you are accustomed to making it, you'll want to try your own variation.

2½ to 3 cups bread flour
1 envelope fast-rising yeast
1 tablespoon sugar
1 teaspoon salt
⅔ cup 125-degree water
3 tablespoons butter
1 egg
1½ tablespoons Pesto or
Italian pesto sauce
¼ cup sliced black olives
¾ cup shredded mozzarella
cheese
½ cup crumbled Garlic and
Herb Cheese or boursin
cheese
6 ounces smoked ham or
salmon, cut into strips
½ cup chopped pimentos
1 tablespoon chopped drained
sun-dried tomatoes
1 egg, beaten
1 tablespoon water

Combine 1½ cups of the bread flour, yeast, sugar and salt in a large bowl. Add the ⅔ cup water, butter and 1 egg; mix well. Add enough remaining flour ½ cup at a time to make a soft dough. Turn onto a lightly floured surface.

Knead for 10 minutes or until smooth and elastic. Place in a greased bowl, turning to coat the surface. Let rise, covered with plastic wrap, until doubled in bulk. Roll the dough into a 10x14-inch rectangle on a lightly floured surface. Place on a greased baking sheet.

Spread pesto down the center third of the dough lengthwise. Sprinkle with the olives, mozzarella cheese and the Garlic and Herb Cheese. Top with the ham strips. Sprinkle with pimentos and sun-dried tomatoes. Cut each side of the dough into 1 inch diagonal strips; fold alternately over the center to enclose the filling. Let rise, uncovered, in a warm place for 30 minutes.

Preheat the oven to 400 degrees.

Brush the loaf with a mixture of 1 egg and 1 tablespoon water. Bake at 400 degrees for 25 minutes or until golden brown. Invert onto a wire rack to cool.

Note: May substitute sun-dried tomato bits for those packed in oil. Blanch in boiling water for 1 minute and drain before using.

Garlic and Herb Cheese

Pesto

Combine the basil, garlic and walnuts in a food processor. Process until finely chopped. Add the olive oil in a fine stream, processing constantly until of a mayonnaise-type consistency. Add the Romano cheese, Parmesan cheese, pepper and salt; mix well.

Garlic and Herb Cheese

Process the cream cheese, butter and garlic in a food processor until smooth. Add the herbs, salt and pepper; mix well.

Spoon into an airtight container. Store, tightly covered, in the refrigerator for 1 week.

Pesto
2 cups fresh basil leaves
4 medium garlic cloves, chopped
1 cup pine nuts or walnuts
1 cup olive oil
¼ cup grated Romano cheese
1 cup grated Parmesan cheese
Freshly ground pepper and salt to taste

Garlic and Herb Cheese
16 ounces cream cheese, softened
2 cups butter, softened
3 to 4 garlic cloves, chopped
3 tablespoons chopped fresh herbs such as basil, chives, marjoram or thyme
Salt and freshly ground pepper to taste

Yield: 1 loaf

Lemon Tea Bread

A Southern classic, this delectable, moist bread is good almost any time, but is especially welcome at coffees, teas and luncheons.

8 ounces cream cheese, softened
1/3 cup butter
1 1/4 cups sugar
2 eggs
2 1/4 cups flour
1 tablespoon baking powder
1/2 teaspoon salt
3/4 cup milk
2 teaspoons grated lemon rind
2/3 cup finely chopped blanched almonds, toasted

Lemon Glaze
2/3 cup sifted confectioners' sugar
2 tablespoons lemon juice
1 teaspoon grated lemon rind

Yield: 2 loaves

Preheat the oven to 350 degrees.

Combine the cream cheese and butter in a large bowl and beat at high speed until light and fluffy. Add the sugar gradually, beating constantly. Add eggs 1 at a time, beating well after each addition.

Mix the flour, baking powder and salt together. Add to the cream cheese mixture alternately with the milk, beginning and ending with the flour mixture and mixing well after each addition.

Stir in 2 teaspoons lemon rind and the almonds. Pour the batter into 2 greased and floured 5x7-inch loaf pans.

Bake at 350 degrees for 50 minutes.

Spoon the Lemon Glaze over the warm loaves. Cool in the pans for 10 minutes; remove to a wire rack to cool completely.

Lemon Glaze

Combine the confectioners' sugar and lemon juice in a small bowl, stirring until smooth. Add the remaining 1 teaspoon lemon rind.

Poppy Seed Bread

This bread is delicious and rich. Be prepared to share the recipe.

Preheat the oven to 350 degrees.

Combine the flour, salt, baking powder, eggs, milk, oil, sugar, poppy seeds and flavorings in a large bowl; beat until well mixed.

Pour the batter into 3 greased small loaf pans.

Bake at 350 degrees for 30 to 35 minutes or until bread tests done. Punch holes in the tops of the loaves. Pour the Orange and Almond Glaze over the hot bread loaves in the pans.

Orange and Almond Glaze

Combine the orange juice, sugar and flavorings in a medium bowl; mix well.

3 cups flour
1½ teaspoons salt
1½ teaspoons baking powder
3 eggs
1½ cups milk
1 cup plus 2 tablespoons vegetable oil
2¼ cups sugar
2 tablespoons poppy seeds
1½ teaspoons vanilla extract
1½ teaspoons butter extract
1½ teaspoons almond extract

Orange and Almond Glaze
¼ cup orange juice
¾ cup sugar
½ teaspoon vanilla extract
½ teaspoon butter extract
½ teaspoon almond extract

Yield: 3 small loaves

Sourdough Bread

One of life's pleasures is warm homemade bread. These luscious sourdough loaves are from Alabama's own Sister Schubert. These and her other wonderful rolls are in your local grocery store.

Original Sourdough Starter

2 envelopes dry yeast

2½ cups warm water, divided

1⅓ cups sugar

6 tablespoons instant potato flakes

Sourdough Bread

1 cup sourdough starter

½ cup melted shortening

1½ cups warm water

1 teaspoon salt

6 cups flour

¼ cup melted butter

Yield: 2 loaves

Original Sourdough Starter

Dissolve the yeast in the ½ cup warm water in a bowl. Stir in the 1 cup warm water, ⅔ cup of the sugar and 3 tablespoons of the potato flakes. Let stand at room temperature for 8 to 12 hours. Chill for 2 to 5 days.

Add the remaining 1 cup warm water, remaining sugar and remaining potato flakes. Let stand for 8 to 12 hours.

Use 1 cup of the starter to make fresh bread. Chill the remaining starter until needed. Continue by adding 1 cup warm water, ⅔ cup sugar and 3 tablespoons potato flakes to feed the dough once a week to keep the starter active.

Sourdough Bread

Combine the starter, shortening, warm water, salt and flour in a large bowl; mix until the batter is stiff. Let rise, covered, for 8 to 12 hours in a warm place.

Punch the dough down and knead slightly. Divide into 2 portions. Knead on a floured surface until smooth and elastic. Shape into loaves or roll out and cut into dinner rolls. Place in 2 greased loaf pans or on baking sheets. Brush the tops with the butter. Let stand, covered, for 6 hours or until the dough rises above the pans.

Preheat the oven to 325 degrees. Bake at 325 degrees for 45 minutes. Remove to a wire rack to cool. May be frozen.

Strawberry Bread

More like cake than bread, this tempting favorite is even better with cream cheese.

Preheat the oven to 350 degrees.

Combine the undrained strawberries, eggs and oil in a medium bowl; mix well.

Add 2½ cups flour, baking soda, salt, cinnamon and sugar; mix well. Toss the pecans in a bowl with the remaining ½ cup flour. Add to the strawberry mixture; mix well.

Pour the batter into 2 greased and floured 5x9-inch loaf pans or three 4x8-inch loaf pans.

Bake at 350 degrees for 50 to 60 minutes or until a cake tester inserted in the center comes out clean.

Cover the top loosely with tent-shaped foil if necessary to prevent overbrowning.

2 (10-ounce) packages frozen
   strawberries, thawed
4 eggs
1¼ cups vegetable oil
3 cups flour
1 teaspoon baking soda
½ teaspoon salt
1 tablespoon cinnamon
2 cups sugar
1 cup chopped pecans

*Yield: 2 loaves or
3 small loaves*

Old World Whole Wheat and

*W*alnuts and wheat bread go together well. *Offer this chewy dark bread in a basket along with a more delicate white bread.*

1 envelope dry yeast
2 teaspoons sugar
2½ cups warm water
1 tablespoon salt
¼ cup finely ground walnuts
3½ cups whole wheat flour
2 to 2½ cups unbleached flour
1½ cups broken walnuts
Cornmeal
¼ teaspoon salt
¼ cup cold water

Yield: 2 loaves

Dissolve the yeast and the sugar in ½ cup of the warm water in a small bowl. Let stand in a warm place for 10 minutes or until the mixture begins to froth.

Combine the remaining 2 cups water and 1 tablespoon salt in a large bowl. Stir in the ground walnuts and the yeast mixture. Add 3 cups of the whole wheat flour 1 cup at a time, mixing well after each addition.

Add the remaining ½ cup whole wheat flour and 1 cup or more of the unbleached flour ½ cup at a time, mixing until the dough pulls from the side of the bowl.

Turn the dough onto a floured surface. Knead for about 10 minutes, adding the remaining unbleached flour. Knead until the dough is resilient and has lost most of its stickiness.

Scatter the broken walnuts on the work surface. Knead into the dough for about 2 minutes.

Place the dough in an oiled bowl, turning to coat the surface. Let rise, covered, for 1 hour or until doubled in bulk.

Punch the dough down. Knead for 1 to 2 minutes and divide the dough into 2 equal portions. Shape each portion into a round ball and place on a baking sheet dusted with cornmeal. Let rise for 45 minutes or until doubled in bulk.

Walnut Loaves

Preheat the oven to 400 degrees.

Slash the top of each loaf to a depth of ½ inch in a crisscross pattern or a row of slashes, using a very sharp knife or razor blade. Do not compress the surface of the risen bread.

Bake at 400 degrees for 20 minutes on the middle oven rack, turning the baking sheet once during baking. Brush the loaves with a mixture of ¼ teaspoon salt dissolved in the cold water. Reduce the oven temperature to 350 degrees. Bake for 30 minutes longer, brushing every 10 minutes with the saltwater. The loaves should be browned and sound hollow when tapped.

Remove the loaves from the baking sheet to a wire rack to cool completely before slicing.

May serve the bread warm by reheating at 300 degrees.

Serve with Herb Butter if desired.

Herb Butter

Cream the butter in a mixer bowl. Stir in the chives, parsley, tarragon, salt and white pepper. Add the mustard; mix well.

Note: May substitute 1 teaspoon fresh lemon juice and a small amount of lemon zest for the mustard.

Herb Butter
½ cup unsalted butter, softened
1 tablespoon finely chopped chives
2 tablespoons finely chopped Italian flat parsley
1 tablespoon finely chopped French tarragon
⅛ teaspoon salt
⅛ teaspoon white pepper
1 teaspoon whole-grain mustard

Cream Biscuits with Blackberry Jam

This is an easy recipe that makes perfect biscuits every time. Cut into smaller shapes for great party biscuits.

1½ cups self-rising flour
1 cup whipping cream
¼ teaspoon baking powder

Blackberry Jam
4 cups fresh blackberries
3 cups sugar

Yield: 2 dozen

Preheat the oven to 450 degrees.

Combine the flour, whipping cream and baking powder in a large bowl; mix well.

Turn the dough onto a lightly floured surface and knead briefly. Roll out the dough and cut with a floured biscuit cutter. Place on an ungreased baking sheet.

Bake at 450 degrees for 10 to 12 minutes or until the biscuits are light brown.

Serve with Blackberry Jam.

Blackberry Jam

Combine blackberries and sugar in a saucepan. Cook over low heat until the sugar is completely dissolved. Bring to a full rolling boil, stirring frequently to prevent sticking. Boil until a small amount of the mixture dropped on a plate will stay in place. Spoon hot mixture into hot sterilized jars; seal with 2-piece lids.

Lemon Cranberry Muffins

Fresh or frozen cranberries may be used. Substitute orange rind for the lemon rind for a subtly different taste.

Preheat the oven to 400 degrees.

Combine the cranberries and 2 tablespoons sugar in a bowl; set aside.

Sift the flour, ½ cup sugar, baking powder and salt into a large bowl. Beat the egg, milk and oil in a small bowl. Add to the flour mixture; stir just until moistened.

Add the cranberry mixture and lemon rind; mix well. Fill greased muffin cups ⅔ full.

Bake at 400 degrees for 20 minutes. Spoon the Lemon Glaze over the warm muffins.

Lemon Glaze

Combine the lemon juice, confectioners' sugar and lemon rind in a small bowl; mix well.

1 cup chopped fresh
    cranberries
2 tablespoons sugar
2 cups flour
½ cup sugar
1 tablespoon baking powder
Salt to taste
1 egg
¾ cup milk
⅓ cup vegetable oil
2 teaspoons grated lemon rind

Lemon Glaze
1 tablespoon lemon juice
½ cup confectioners' sugar
1 tablespoon grated lemon
    rind

Yield: 1 dozen

Russell Hill Rolls

Everyone loves these feather-light rolls. Serve them with your favorite dinner or with tenderloin or ham for a cocktail buffet. They freeze beautifully.

2 envelopes dry yeast
¼ cup lukewarm water
1 teaspoon salt
½ cup sugar
2 tablespoons (rounded) shortening
1 cup boiling water
1 egg, beaten
4 cups flour, sifted
Melted butter

Yield: 4 dozen

Dissolve the yeast in the lukewarm water in a small bowl; set aside.

Combine the salt, sugar and shortening in a medium bowl; mix well. Pour the boiling water over the mixture and let cool. Add the egg and yeast; mix well. Add the flour gradually, mixing well after each addition.

Let rise, covered, for 1 hour. Knead the dough on a lightly floured surface until smooth and elastic. Place in a greased bowl, turning to coat the surface. Chill, covered, in the refrigerator overnight.

Roll the dough on a floured surface; cut with a biscuit cutter. Brush with melted butter; fold over and place on a nonstick baking sheet. Let rise in a warm place for 2 hours or until doubled in bulk.

Preheat the oven to 400 degrees. Bake at 400 degrees for 15 minutes or until golden brown.

Sour Cream Crescent Rolls

Start these pretty dinner rolls the night before they are to be served.

Heat the sour cream in a double boiler over simmering water until slightly yellow around the edge. Dissolve the yeast in warm water in a small bowl; let stand for 5 to 10 minutes.

Combine 1 cup butter, sugar and salt in a large bowl. Add the hot sour cream; mix until the butter is completely melted. Let the mixture cool to lukewarm.

Blend in 1 cup of the flour. Add the yeast and 1 cup of the flour; beat until smooth. Add the eggs and remaining 2 cups flour; beat until smooth. Chill, covered, for 6 hours to overnight.

Divide the dough into 4 portions. Roll each portion into a ¼-inch thick circle on a lightly floured surface. Cut into 12 wedges. Roll wedges from the wide end. Shape into crescents on a greased baking sheet. Let rise, uncovered, in a warm place for 1 hour or longer.

Preheat the oven to 375 degrees. Brush rolls with the melted butter. Bake at 375 degrees for 15 minutes or until the rolls are a light golden brown.

1 cup sour cream
1½ envelopes dry yeast
⅓ cup warm water
1 cup butter or margarine, softened
½ cup sugar
½ teaspoon salt
4 cups flour, sifted
2 eggs, beaten
3 tablespoons melted butter

Yield: 4 dozen

Sweet Country Cornbread

$\mathcal{T}$his cornbread is delicious toasted with a little butter. Cornbread is a requirement for any Southern vegetable dinner. The sugar may be reduced if a less sweet cornbread is preferred.

2 cups self-rising cornmeal
½ cup flour
⅓ cup sugar
2 cups buttermilk
½ cup melted shortening

Yield: 8 servings

Preheat the oven to 425 degrees.

Combine the cornmeal, flour, sugar and buttermilk in a bowl; mix well.

Melt the shortening in a large cast-iron skillet. Pour the hot shortening into the batter; mix well. Pour the batter into the hot skillet.

Bake at 425 degrees for approximately 30 minutes or until golden brown. Invert onto a serving plate.

My mother said, "The day may come when all we can offer is well water and cold cornbread, but at least we'll be able to serve it on a table set with proper linen."

Truman Capote
The Thanksgiving Visitor

Fan Window

Chip Cooper

*The extraordinary leaded glass fanlight over the entrance to the
1819 Weeden House Museum is but one of its stunning architectural
features. Once the home of renowned Huntsville poet and artist,
Maria Howard Weeden, it is Alabama's oldest house museum.*

This photograph was underwritten by Katherine Bagby Robertson, President 1966–1967; Ruth Owen Franklin Lee, President, 1974–1975

Photograph right:
Roasted Peppers with
Herbed Goat Cheese
Grilled Lamb Kabobs
Grilled Pineapple with Kirsch

Overleaf:
Herb Vinegars

Side Dishes

~~~~~

Alabama, they say,
is like one big front porch
where folks gather on
summer nights to tell tales
and to talk family.

—Kathryn Tucker Windham
Alabama: One Big Front Porch

This photograph was underwritten by Virginia King Griffith, President 1984–1985

Artichokes with Basil Béarnaise

*A spectacular presentation—nature has
done the work for you.*

Rinse the artichokes, slice off the stems so the artichokes can stand level and remove any tough outer leaves. Slice off the top inch of each artichoke and rub the exposed area with the lemon. Snip off the top half inch of each leaf. Rub all cut surfaces with the lemon.

Place the artichokes base side down in boiling water in a stockpot; reduce heat to medium. Weight the artichokes with a lid that fits into the stockpot to keep the artichokes submerged. Simmer for 30 to 40 minutes or until the base can be pierced easily with a knife point. Do not undercook. Drain upside down.

Scoop out the inner leaves and the fuzzy choke, taking care not to remove any of the fleshy bottom beneath. Place the artichokes in a dish, cover with a clean towel wrung out in hot water and set aside to keep warm.

Spoon about ¼ cup of the warm Basil Béarnaise into the center of each warm artichoke.

Basil Béarnaise

Combine 2 tablespoons of the vermouth with the vinegar in a saucepan. Add the shallots. Cook for 5 minutes or until the shallots are tender and the liquid is reduced to 1 tablespoon. Stir in the remaining 1 tablespoon of vermouth. Strain.

Whisk the egg yolks in a bowl until thickened. Whisk the vermouth mixture into the egg yolks.

Place the egg yolk mixture in a double boiler over hot water. Add the melted butter gradually, beating constantly. Cook until the sauce is thickened, stirring constantly. Season with salt and pepper; stir in the basil. May keep the sauce warm in a double boiler over simmering water.

4 large globe artichokes
1 lemon, cut into halves

Basil Béarnaise
3 tablespoons dry vermouth
*3 tablespoons white wine
    vinegar*
1 tablespoon minced shallots
2 egg yolks
¾ cup melted unsalted butter
*Salt and freshly ground white
    pepper to taste*
*¼ cup minced fresh basil
    leaves*

Yield: 4 servings

Broccoli and Cheese Strudel

A cheesy broccoli filling encased in a beautiful golden crust.

2 pounds fresh broccoli or spinach
½ cup boiling water
½ cup finely chopped onion
¼ cup butter
3 eggs
2 cups feta cheese, crumbled
¼ cup chopped parsley
2 tablespoons chopped fresh dill
½ teaspoon salt
Pepper to taste
10 frozen phyllo pastry sheets, thawed
½ cup melted butter

Yield: 8 servings

Preheat the oven to 350 degrees.

Rinse the broccoli and pat dry; trim and discard the stem ends. Split the stalks and chop the stems and florets.

Place the broccoli in the boiling water in a large saucepan. Cook, covered, over medium heat for 5 minutes. Remove from heat and drain well.

Sauté the onion in ¼ cup butter in a large skillet for about 3 minutes or until golden brown. Add the chopped broccoli. Sauté for 1 minute longer, stirring constantly. Beat the eggs in a large bowl. Add the cheese, broccoli mixture, parsley, dill, salt and pepper; mix well.

Line the inside of a 9-inch springform pan with 6 of the pastry sheets, overlapping the edges and brushing each sheet with melted butter.

Pour the broccoli mixture into the pan. Fold the overlapping edges of the pastry sheets over the top of the mixture.

Cut four 9-inch circles from the remaining 4 phyllo sheets with scissors. Brush each circle with melted butter, then layer over the top of the mixture. Slice through the pastry circles to mark 8 wedges. Pour any remaining melted butter over the top.

Place the springform pan on a larger pan to catch the drippings. Bake at 350 degrees for 40 to 45 minutes or until the crust is puffy and golden brown. Remove to a wire rack to cool.

Note: May substitute three 10-ounce packages frozen broccoli for the fresh broccoli.

Marinated Chick-Peas and Asparagus

*A*sparagus and chick-peas add a lively twist to the classic combination of feta cheese, tomatoes and black olives in this colorful concoction.

Sweet Garlic Marinade

Whip the sugar, garlic, salt and pepper into the vinegar in a large bowl. Add the oil gradually, whipping constantly. Stir in the sesame seeds.

Chick-Peas and Asparagus

Steam the asparagus in a steamer for 6 to 8 minutes or until tender-crisp. Cool and cut into 1½-inch pieces.

Toss the asparagus, cheese, chick-peas, tomatoes, green onions and olives gently in a medium bowl. Pour the Sweet Garlic Marinade over the asparagus mixture. Chill, covered, for 48 hours.

Stir the pecans into the vegetables and marinade mixture. Spoon over the lettuce leaves on salad plates. Drizzle with desired amount of Sweet Garlic Marinade.

Note: May substitute one 11-ounce can drained mandarin oranges for the tomatoes.

Sweet Garlic Marinade

8 teaspoons sugar

1 clove of garlic, minced

¼ teaspoon salt

⅛ teaspoon white pepper

½ cup white wine vinegar

¾ cup walnut oil

1 tablespoon (heaping) toasted sesame seeds

Chick-Peas and Asparagus

1 bunch small fresh asparagus stalks

½ cup feta cheese, crumbled

1 (16-ounce) can chick-peas, drained

3 or 4 Roma tomatoes, quartered

½ cup thinly sliced green onions

⅓ cup sliced black olives

1 cup toasted pecan pieces

Romaine lettuce leaves, torn into bite-size pieces

Yield: 8 servings

Side Dishes

Red Cabbage Braised in White Wine

Slow braising in wine gives cabbage a fresh taste and a tender-firm texture. Delicious served with pork and red potatoes.

4 slices bacon, cut into small pieces
2 tablespoons olive oil
1 carrot, chopped
¾ cup white wine
1 head red cabbage, cored, quartered, sliced into ½-inch strips
1 teaspoon dried thyme
2 teaspoons salt
Finely ground pepper to taste
2 teaspoons (or more) red wine vinegar
Goat cheese or bleu cheese, crumbled (optional)

Yield: 8 servings

Sauté the bacon in olive oil in a large saucepan for 3 minutes. Add the carrot and wine. Heat just until the mixture begins to simmer.

Add the cabbage to the saucepan, sprinkling it with thyme, salt and pepper.

Cook, covered, over low heat for 30 to 40 minutes, stirring 2 to 3 times. Add the vinegar and stir. Cook for 2 to 3 minutes longer.

Crumble the cheese over the top of the cabbage immediately before serving.

Wild Mushrooms Marsala with Yellow Grits

*G*rits have more character than other starches and absorb all the succulent juices from the sautéed mushrooms. This imaginative combination also makes an excellent first course.

Bring the water and salt to a boil in a medium saucepan. Stir in the grits. Cook for 30 minutes over low heat, adding more water as necessary. Spoon into a greased baking pan.

Chill for 1 hour or until the grits are cool and firm.

Preheat the broiler.

Cut the grits into 1x3-inch strips, rub with butter and heat in the broiler. Place the grits on a warm serving plate; spoon the Wild Mushrooms Marsala over the top.

Wild Mushrooms Marsala

Soak the dried mushrooms in warm water to cover in a small bowl for 1 hour. Drain the mushrooms, reserving ¼ cup of the liquid.

Melt the butter in a skillet and add the fresh mushrooms and shallots. Sauté over low heat. Add the lemon juice, dried mushrooms and marsala. Cook until the liquid is reduced. Add the reserved mushroom liquid; mix well. Add the thyme, parsley, salt and pepper.

3 cups water

1½ teaspoons salt

1 cup coarsely ground yellow grits

Softened butter

Wild Mushrooms Marsala

½ ounce dried wild mushrooms

2 tablespoons butter

½ cup fresh mushrooms

½ tablespoon shallots

1 tablespoon lemon juice

¼ cup sweet marsala

3 small sprigs of fresh thyme

Parsley to taste

Salt and pepper to taste

Yield: 8 servings

Vidalia Onion Casserole

ven people who don't like onions like this outstanding casserole. Especially good with beef, pork or lamb. Add a good red wine for an opulent dinner.

4 large Vidalia onions,
sliced ½ inch thick
½ cup butter
½ cup beef broth
½ cup sherry
2 tablespoons flour
1½ cups seasoned soft
bread crumbs
½ cup shredded sharp
Cheddar cheese
¼ cup grated Parmesan
cheese

Yield: 6 servings

Preheat the oven to 350 degrees.

Sauté the onions in the butter in a skillet over low heat until the onions become translucent.

Add the beef broth, sherry and flour; mix well. Cook until slightly thickened, stirring constantly. Spoon the mixture into a greased medium casserole.

Sprinkle the bread crumbs, Cheddar cheese and Parmesan cheese over the onion mixture.

Bake at 350 degrees for 20 minutes or until light brown and bubbly.

Grilled Peppers with Eggplant

The flavors of summer—red peppers stuffed with fresh basil, eggplant, garlic and onion.

Preheat the grill.

Salt each slice of eggplant and place in a bowl. Let stand for 30 minutes. Rinse the eggplant; pat dry and cut into cubes.

Sauté the garlic and onion in the olive oil in a medium skillet. Add the eggplant. Cook over medium heat for 5 minutes or until tender.

Combine the eggplant mixture with the bread crumbs, cheese, hot pepper sauce, egg, Worcestershire sauce, basil and parsley in a large bowl; mix well.

Slice the tops off the red peppers, reserving the tops. Discard the seeds; rinse and pat the peppers dry. Polish the peppers and tops with a small amount of olive oil. Sprinkle a small amount of salt inside each pepper.

Stuff each pepper with the eggplant mixture and 1 teaspoon butter. Place the tops on the stuffed peppers and secure with wooden picks.

Grill the peppers for 40 minutes or until tender.

Note: May substitute 2 tablespoons finely chopped curly parsley and 2 tablespoons finely chopped cilantro for the Italian flat-leaf parsley.

Salt to taste
1 medium eggplant, peeled, sliced
2 cloves of garlic, minced
1 chopped onion
¼ cup olive oil
1 cup bread crumbs
½ to ¾ cup grated Parmesan cheese
Hot pepper sauce to taste
1 egg, beaten
Worcestershire sauce to taste
¼ cup finely chopped sweet basil leaves
¼ cup finely chopped Italian flat-leaf parsley
4 red bell peppers
4 teaspoons butter

Yield: 4 servings

Dijon Potatoes

From the scalloped potato family but even better. The fresh herbs and Dijon mustard superbly flavor the creamy sauce.

3¼ pounds potatoes, peeled,
thinly sliced
½ cup plus 2 tablespoons
butter
7 tablespoons water
Salt and pepper to taste
1½ tablespoons finely
chopped fresh parsley
1½ tablespoons finely
chopped fresh chervil
1½ tablespoons finely
chopped sweet basil
1½ tablespoons finely
chopped fresh chives
5 teaspoons Dijon mustard

Crème Fraîche
3 tablespoons sour cream
7 tablespoons whipping
cream
Salt and pepper to taste

Yield: 6 servings

Sauté the potatoes in the butter in a large skillet until golden brown. Add the water, salt and pepper. Cook, covered, over low heat for 20 minutes.

Combine the parsley, chervil, basil, chives, Crème Fraîche and mustard in a medium bowl and blend lightly.

Spoon the potatoes into a warmed 9x13-inch serving dish and top with the sauce.

Crème Fraîche

Combine the sour cream and the whipping cream in a medium bowl. Add salt and pepper; mix well.

Squash Puppies

Hush puppies with a delightful difference.

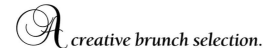

Preheat the oil in a deep fryer to 350 degrees.

Trim ends off the squash; slice and place in a saucepan. Cover squash with water. Cook over medium heat for 20 minutes or until tender. Drain squash well; mash and drain again.

Combine the squash and the remaining ingredients in a bowl. Drop by scant tablespoonfuls into 350-degree oil in a deep fryer. Deep-fry for 5 minutes or until golden brown.

5 medium yellow squash
1 egg, beaten
½ cup buttermilk
1 medium onion, chopped
¾ cup self-rising cornmeal
¼ cup flour

Yield: about 2½ dozen

Herbed Spinach Stuffing

A creative brunch selection.

Drain the spinach. Combine with the stuffing mix, cheese, eggs, butter and nutmeg; mix well. Shape into 2½-inch balls using an ice cream scoop. Place on a baking sheet lined with waxed paper.

Chill, covered, for 8 hours.

Preheat the oven to 350 degrees. Place the spinach balls on a lightly greased baking sheet. Bake at 350 degrees for 15 minutes.

Arrange the spinach balls on red pepper rings on a serving platter. If desired, serve with the Gourmet Hot Mustard as a sauce, page 17.

2 (10-ounce) packages frozen
* chopped spinach, thawed*
2 cups herb-seasoned stuffing
* mix, crushed*
1 cup grated Parmesan cheese
6 eggs, beaten
½ cup butter, softened
Ground nutmeg to taste
Sweet red bell pepper rings

Yield: 8 servings

Harvest Acorn Squash

A sweet and showy accompaniment to a pork or poultry main dish.

½ cup chopped dried apricots

1½ cups cooked yellow squash

1½ cups cream

6 tablespoons brown sugar

2 tablespoons sugar

1 teaspoon cinnamon

½ teaspoon ginger

⅛ teaspoon cloves

½ cup dark corn syrup

4 acorn squash, cut into halves, seeded

2 tablespoons toasted pumpkin seeds

Yield: 4 servings

Preheat the oven to 350 degrees.

Combine the apricots, yellow squash, cream, brown sugar, sugar, cinnamon, ginger, cloves and corn syrup in a double boiler; mix well. Cook over hot water until thickened, stirring constantly.

Poach the acorn squash in ¼ inch of water in a saucepan for 5 minutes; drain. Place the acorn squash on a lightly greased baking sheet. Spoon the apricot mixture into the acorn squash.

Bake at 350 degrees for 30 minutes or until tender.

Sprinkle with toasted pumpkin seeds just before serving.

Stuffed Zucchini

Rich and cheesy—a vegetable dish no one can resist.

Cook the zucchini in boiling water in a saucepan for 10 minutes. Drain and cut into halves lengthwise. Scoop out the centers and chop, leaving a ¼-inch shell.

Preheat the broiler.

Melt the butter in a large skillet. Add the mushrooms. Sauté until tender. Stir in the flour and oregano and remove from heat. Add the Monterey Jack cheese and pimento. Add the chopped zucchini; mix well. Cook over low heat until heated through, stirring often.

Fill the zucchini shells with the mushroom mixture. Sprinkle with the Parmesan cheese.

Broil in an 8x10-inch casserole for 3 to 5 minutes or until the cheese is hot and bubbly.

May be assembled and chilled for up to 4 hours before serving and broiled for 5 to 7 minutes.

3 medium zucchini
2 tablespoons butter
1 cup chopped fresh
   mushrooms
2 tablespoons flour
¼ teaspoon dried oregano,
   crushed
1 cup shredded Monterey
   Jack cheese
2 tablespoons chopped
   pimento
¼ cup grated Parmesan
   cheese

Yield: 4 servings

Sweet Potato Soufflé

__T__his will become a family Thanksgiving favorite.

3 cups peeled, quartered,
cooked sweet potatoes
1 teaspoon vanilla extract
¼ teaspoon salt
1¼ cups sugar
½ cup butter
2 teaspoons baking powder
3 eggs, beaten

Brown Sugar Topping
⅓ cup butter, softened
½ cup packed brown sugar
3 cups crushed cornflakes
½ cup chopped pecans

Yield: 6 servings

Preheat the oven to 400 degrees. Combine the sweet potatoes, vanilla, salt, sugar, butter, baking powder and eggs in a large bowl; beat until smooth and creamy. Spoon into a greased baking dish.

Bake at 400 degrees for 20 minutes.

Sprinkle the Brown Sugar Topping over the sweet potatoes. Bake for 10 minutes longer.

Brown Sugar Topping

Cream the butter and brown sugar in a small bowl. Add the cornflakes; mix well. Add the chopped pecans and stir until the mixture is crumbly.

Festive Tomatoes

*I*t's amazing what these colorful, spinach-stuffed
tomatoes add to a plate's appeal. A beautiful
and classic accompaniment to a roast.

Preheat the oven to 350 degrees.

Combine the flour and the half-and-half in a small bowl;
mix well and set aside. Rinse the spinach, drain and pat dry. Tear
into bite-size pieces.

Scoop the pulp from the tomatoes, keeping tomato shells
intact; drain. Place the tomatoes in a shallow baking dish sprayed
with nonstick cooking spray.

Bake at 350 degrees for 5 to 10 minutes or just until tender
but not mushy.

Sauté the garlic in the olive oil in a medium skillet over low
heat. Add the spinach gradually. Sauté until tender.

Add the Monterey Jack cheese. Cook until the cheese melts,
stirring constantly. Add the flour mixture, salt and pepper. Cook
until thickened and creamy, stirring constantly.

Fill the tomatoes with the spinach mixture. Sprinkle with
additional Monterey Jack cheese, Parmesan cheese and bread
crumbs. Bake at 350 degrees for 15 to 20 minutes or until the
tomatoes are heated through and the cheese is bubbly. Top with
the fresh parsley sprigs and sprinkle with paprika.

Note: May use frozen spinach if fresh spinach is not
available.

1 teaspoon flour
2 tablespoons half-and-half
*1 (16-ounce) package fresh
    spinach*
4 large tomatoes, cored
1 clove of garlic, crushed
2 tablespoons olive oil
*1½ cups shredded Monterey
    Jack cheese*
Salt and pepper to taste
*⅓ cup grated fresh Parmesan
    cheese*
¾ cup seasoned bread crumbs
Parsley sprigs
Paprika to taste

Yield: 4 servings

Fried Green Tomatoes

A Southern specialty that was not widely known outside the region until Alabama's Fannie Flagg wrote "Fried Green Tomatoes at the Whistle Stop Cafe" and made it a popular item.

3 to 4 large green tomatoes
2 cups yellow cornmeal
2 tablespoons flour
1 teaspoon salt
¼ teaspoon cayenne pepper
Vegetable oil for frying

Yield: 6 to 8 servings

Slice the tomatoes approximately ¼ inch thick.

Combine the cornmeal, flour, salt and cayenne pepper in a shallow dish. Dredge the tomatoes in the cornmeal mixture. Heat a cast-iron skillet over high heat until very hot. Add the oil and reduce the heat to medium.

Add the tomatoes. Fry each side until golden brown. Remove from skillet and drain on paper towels. Season the tomatoes with Tabasco sauce or balsamic vinegar if desired.

Great served on grilled hamburgers or your favorite sandwich.

Photograph right:
Heritage Fried Chicken
Fried Green Tomatoes
Stuffed New Potatoes
Cappuccino Brownies
Blackberry Lemonade

Bank at Dusk

Chip Cooper

*On a limestone bluff above historic Big Spring rises this masterful
example of Greek Revival style by noted architect George Steele.
The commanding structure, which first opened its doors for banking
in 1835, is all that remains of Huntsville's famed Cotton Row.*

Photograph right:
Prosciutto and Portobello
Mushroom Lasagna
French Bread

Overleaf:
Warm Asian Beef and Pasta

Pasta

❧

*It was a rich life.
Even I, the most selfish and
least satisfied and most sensitive
and wary one, even I knew
I was living in a blessed time.*

—Ellen Gilchrist
Net of Jewels

This photograph was underwritten by Butch Kohler Damson, President 1977–1978

Summer Garden Tomato Sauce

The earthy goodness of basic tomato sauce is enlivened here with fresh eggplant. Create your own variations using your favorite garden herbs and vegetables.

Sprinkle a pinch of salt on eggplant slices in a bowl. Let stand for 30 minutes. Pat dry with paper towels. Cut into cubes. Sauté the garlic and onions in the olive oil in a very large skillet over medium heat until golden brown.

Add the tomatoes, red bell peppers, eggplant, carrots, bay leaves, chile pepper, parsley, basil, salt, pepper and sugar; mix well. Reduce the heat; simmer for 1 hour. Remove the bay leaves.

Note: May store the sauce in an airtight container in the freezer. May substitute green or yellow bell peppers for the red bell peppers if desired.

Salt to taste

2 medium eggplant, unpeeled, sliced into ½-inch strips

4 cloves of garlic, coarsely chopped

4 medium white onions, coarsely chopped

2 to 3 tablespoons extra-virgin olive oil

4 to 5 pounds Italian plum tomatoes, peeled, coarsely chopped

2 red bell peppers, chopped

2 carrots, peeled, thinly sliced

2 bay leaves

1 hot chile pepper, finely chopped

1 large bunch fresh Italian parsley

1 cup sweet basil leaves

Pepper to taste

Sugar to taste

Yield: 12 servings

Capellini with Shrimp

Whether you are on vacation or just dreaming about the ocean, this will satisfy your seafood yearnings.

½ cup fresh parsley, finely chopped
3 cloves of garlic, finely chopped
32 ounces Italian plum tomatoes, chopped
½ cup plus 1 tablespoon olive oil
1 teaspoon dried oregano
Salt and pepper to taste
2 cups chopped fresh basil
2 pounds medium or small shrimp, sliced lengthwise
8 ounces uncooked capellini
Fresh parsley for garnish

Yield: 4 servings as an entrée

Combine the parsley, two-thirds of the garlic and the tomatoes with ½ cup of the olive oil and the oregano in a large skillet; mix well. Stir in salt and pepper. Cook over medium heat for 10 minutes. Mix the basil with 2 teaspoons of the olive oil. Add to the sauce; mix well.

Sprinkle the shrimp with salt. Heat the remaining garlic in the remaining 1 teaspoon olive oil in a skillet. Remove the garlic. Add the shrimp to the skillet. Sauté for 2 minutes.

Stir in the tomato sauce.

Cook the capellini in boiling water to cover in a saucepan for 3 minutes. Rinse in cold water; drain well.

Toss the sauce with the capellini in a serving bowl. Garnish with parsley and sprinkle with pepper.

Chicken Marsala on Angel Hair Pasta

Marsala wine lends this simple chicken dish a slightly sweet, rich and complex flavor and a wonderful aroma.

Rinse the chicken and pat dry. Coat the chicken in the seasoned flour in a bowl.

Melt the butter in a medium skillet. Add the chicken. Cook over medium heat for 4 minutes on each side or until cooked through, reserving the pan drippings for the sauce.

Arrange the chicken on a bed of angel hair pasta on a serving platter. Spoon the Marsala Sauce on top.

Marsala Sauce

Sauté the mushrooms in the reserved pan drippings in a skillet. Add the chicken broth, marsala and pepper. Add a mixture of the cornstarch and water. Cook until thickened, stirring constantly.

Note: Cook the pasta just before serving. Angel hair pasta cooks very quickly since it is so fine in texture.

8 boneless chicken breast
   halves
1 cup seasoned flour
½ cup butter
16 ounces angel hair pasta,
   cooked, drained

Marsala Sauce
3 cups sliced mushrooms
Reserved pan drippings from
   the chicken
1 (10-ounce) can chicken
   broth
½ cup sweet or dry marsala
Freshly ground pepper to taste
1 tablespoon cornstarch
3 tablespoons water

Yield: 4 servings as an entrée, or 8 servings as a first course or side dish

Prosciutto and Portobello Mushroom Lasagna

Chef Chris Sowder's extraordinary lasagna features meaty portobello mushrooms.

½ cup butter
6 tablespoons flour
4 cups milk, scalded
½ teaspoon salt
½ teaspoon nutmeg
½ cup ricotta cheese
½ cup finely chopped onion
¼ cup olive oil
¼ cup butter
½ cup canned Italian plum tomatoes, drained, chopped
2 tablespoons chopped fresh parsley
2 pounds fresh portobello mushrooms, sliced
2 tablespoons butter, softened
1 (12-ounce) package lasagna noodles, cooked, drained
12 ounces prosciutto, cut into strips
⅔ cup freshly grated Parmesan cheese

Yield: 8 servings

Heat ½ cup butter in a saucepan until melted. Stir in the flour. Cook for 3 to 4 minutes or until smooth, stirring constantly. Stir in the milk gradually. Cook until thickened, stirring constantly. Stir in salt and nutmeg. Cook over low heat for 20 minutes, stirring frequently. Add ricotta cheese.

Sauté the onion in the olive oil and ¼ cup butter in a skillet until tender. Stir in the tomatoes and parsley. Cook until most of the liquid has evaporated, stirring frequently. Add the mushrooms; mix well. Cook for 5 to 6 minutes or until of the desired consistency, stirring frequently.

Preheat the oven to 400 degrees.

Spread the sides and bottom of a lasagna pan with 2 tablespoons butter. Layer the noodles, mushroom mixture, white sauce, prosciutto and Parmesan cheese alternately until all the ingredients are used, ending with the noodles.

Bake at 400 degrees for 15 to 20 minutes or until bubbly. Let stand for 10 minutes before serving.

Linguini with Lobster and Lime Sauce

An incredible main dish or an elegant first course.

Place the linguini in a saucepan with boiling water to cover. Cook over medium heat for 5 minutes; drain.

Heat the olive oil and butter in a medium skillet. Add the onion. Sauté just until golden brown. Stir in the garlic, parsley and dill.

Add the tomatoes. Cook for 5 minutes over low heat, stirring occasionally. Stir in the lime juice and brandy; season with salt and white pepper.

Arrange the cooked linguini on 4 warmed individual serving plates.

Add the lobster to the sauce and toss just until heated through. Spoon over the linguini. Garnish with the lime wedges and parsley.

8 ounces uncooked linguini
1 tablespoon olive oil
1 tablespoon butter
½ medium onion, finely chopped
1 large clove of garlic, minced
¼ cup chopped parsley
2 teaspoons dill
2 tomatoes, peeled, chopped
1½ tablespoons fresh lime juice
1 tablespoon brandy (optional)
Salt and white pepper to taste
1½ cups chopped cooked lobster
1 lime, cut into wedges
Parsley to taste

Yield: 4 servings

Linguini with Scallops

arnish with additional fresh parsley to add color.

1 pound fresh bay scallops
2 tablespoons fresh
lemon juice
1 tablespoon chopped parsley
1 large clove of garlic, minced
Dash of freshly grated nutmeg
Dash of ground ginger
Salt and freshly ground white
pepper to taste
16 ounces uncooked linguini
5 tablespoons butter
¼ cup whipping cream
¼ cup freshly grated
Parmesan cheese

Yield: 4 servings

Rinse the scallops in cold water; drain well. Combine the scallops with the lemon juice, parsley, garlic, nutmeg, ginger, salt and white pepper in a bowl; mix well.

Cook the linguini in salted boiling water in a medium saucepan; drain.

Melt the butter in a skillet. Drain the scallops. Add to the skillet. Sauté for 3 to 4 minutes, coating well with the butter.

Add the whipping cream to the scallops. Simmer for 1 minute, stirring constantly.

Combine the linguini with the scallop mixture in a shallow bowl or on a shell-shaped serving platter; toss well.

Sprinkle with the Parmesan cheese. Serve immediately.

Lemon Pasta with Chicken and Zucchini

This satisfying pasta looks and tastes as fresh as it sounds. Try fettuccini as your pasta choice and, as a variation, add thinly sliced mushrooms.

Sauté the zucchini in olive oil in a large skillet until tender. Remove the zucchini from the skillet with a slotted spoon; drain on paper towels.

Add the chicken, onion and garlic to the drippings in the skillet. Cook over medium heat for 8 to 10 minutes or until the chicken is tender, stirring frequently. Stir in the whipping cream. Bring to a boil; reduce heat. Simmer for 5 minutes or until the sauce is reduced by about one-third.

Add the sautéed zucchini, ½ cup of the Parmesan cheese, salt, pepper and the cooked pasta; mix well. Cook until heated through. Serve sprinkled with the remaining ¼ cup Parmesan cheese.

Note: Serving this pasta dish in individual shallow heated serving bowls makes it easier to eat and retains the heat for a longer time.

5 small zucchini, julienned

¼ cup plus 1 tablespoon olive oil

2 (6-ounce) chicken breast halves, skinned, boned, cut into 1-inch pieces

1½ cups chopped onion

1 clove of garlic, crushed

⅔ cup whipping cream

¾ cup freshly grated Parmesan cheese

¼ teaspoon salt

⅛ teaspoon pepper

7 cups cooked lemon-flavored pasta, drained

Yield: 8 servings

Stuffed Manicotti with Crab Meat Sauce

simple mixed green salad, fresh bread and a good wine will round out the menu.

8 (4-ounce) manicotti shells
1½ cups large curd cottage cheese
1 cup grated Parmesan cheese
1 egg, beaten
2 tablespoons chopped parsley

Crab Meat Sauce
1 cup chopped onion
1 clove of garlic, minced
2 tablespoons olive oil
1 (16-ounce) can tomatoes
1 (8-ounce) can tomato sauce
1½ teaspoons basil
½ teaspoon salt
1 pound fresh crab meat, drained, flaked

Yield: 4 servings

Preheat the oven to 350 degrees.

Cook the manicotti shells in boiling water to cover in a saucepan according to package directions; drain. Rinse the manicotti shells in cold water.

Combine the cottage cheese, ½ cup of the Parmesan cheese, egg and parsley in a medium bowl; mix well. Fill the manicotti shells with equal amounts of the cottage cheese mixture. Spoon one-third of the Crab Meat Sauce over the bottom of a shallow 1½-quart casserole. Arrange the filled manicotti shells in the prepared casserole. Top with the remaining Crab Meat Sauce. Cover with foil and crimp to the edge of the casserole.

Bake at 350 degrees for 25 minutes. Bake, uncovered, for 15 minutes longer. Sprinkle with the remaining ½ cup Parmesan cheese before serving.

Crab Meat Sauce

Sauté the onion and garlic in the olive oil in a skillet until the onion is translucent. Add the tomatoes, tomato sauce, basil and salt; mix well. Reduce the heat and simmer, uncovered, for 30 minutes, stirring occasionally.

Stir the crab meat into the sauce. Cook until heated through, stirring constantly.

Ravioli with Ricotta-Parmesan Filling

Make this irresistible, filled pasta for a special occasion.

Combine the egg yolks, egg, water, olive oil and salt in a bowl; mix well. Spoon 1½ cups of the flour into a large bowl. Make a well in the center and add the egg mixture. Stir with a fork until the flour is moistened and well mixed. Pat into a ball.

Sprinkle ¼ cup of the flour onto a flat work surface. Knead the dough for 5 to 10 minutes or until smooth and elastic. Wrap the dough in plastic wrap and refrigerate for 2 hours or until ready to use.

Sprinkle ¼ cup of the flour onto a flat work surface. Divide the dough into 2 portions. Roll 1 portion into a thin large rectangle on the work surface. Drop the Ricotta-Parmesan Filling onto the pasta rectangle by teaspoonfuls 2 to 2½ inches apart. Moisten the area around the Ricotta-Parmesan Filling with a pastry brush dipped in water.

Sprinkle the remaining ¼ cup flour onto a flat work surface. Roll the remaining dough into a thin large rectangle. Press carefully over the filled sheet, sealing firmly at the edges and between the Ricotta-Parmesan Filling. Cut into individual squares using a ravioli cutter or small sharp knife.

Drop the ravioli into boiling water in a large saucepan. Cook for 6 to 8 minutes or until the pasta is soft but still firm; drain well. Spoon the ravioli onto a serving platter. Pour a mixture of butter and garlic over the ravioli. Garnish with Parmesan cheese and serve immediately.

Ricotta-Parmesan Filling

Combine the Swiss chard, ricotta cheese, cream cheese, salt and pepper in a bowl; mix well. Add 2 eggs and Parmesan cheese; mix well.

3 egg yolks
1 egg
2 tablespoons water
1 teaspoon olive oil
½ teaspoon salt
2¼ cups flour
Melted butter to taste
Minced garlic to taste
Additional Parmesan cheese

Ricotta-Parmesan Filling
1 pound Swiss chard or fresh
    spinach, finely chopped,
    cooked, drained
1 cup ricotta cheese
2 ounces cream cheese,
    softened
Salt and freshly ground
    pepper to taste
2 eggs
2 cups grated Parmesan
    cheese

Yield: 4 to 6 servings

San Antonio Pasta with

*A favorite at Vincent's Market in Birmingham,
this hearty dish is a meal in itself.*

12 ounces radiatore pasta
½ red onion, finely chopped
1 zucchini, seeded,
julienned
1 yellow squash,
seeded, julienned
½ pint cherry tomatoes,
cut into halves
½ green bell pepper,
thinly sliced
½ red bell pepper,
thinly sliced
½ yellow bell pepper,
thinly sliced
1 jalapeño, seeded, minced
1 cup shredded Monterey
Jack cheese
⅛ bunch green onions,
finely chopped
⅓ bunch cilantro, chopped,
or to taste

Cook the pasta al dente in boiling water in a large saucepan; drain well. Rinse with cold water.

Combine the onion, zucchini, yellow squash, tomatoes, bell peppers, jalapeño, cheese, green onions and cilantro in a large bowl; mix well. Add the cooked pasta to the vegetable mixture; toss to mix well.

Drizzle the Spicy Lime Dressing over the pasta and vegetables; toss to coat.

Chill, covered, until ready to serve.

Spicy Lime Dressing

Spicy Lime Dressing

Whisk the lime zest, lime juice, sherry, cumin, cardamom, garlic, salt and pepper in a bowl gently. Add the olive oil and soy oil in a fine stream, whisking constantly until well blended.

Spicy Lime Dressing

1/8 teaspoon lime zest

1 1/3 tablespoons lime juice

2 tablespoons plus 1 teaspoon sherry

1 1/2 teaspoons ground cumin

1/2 teaspoon ground cardamom

2 teaspoons chopped garlic

2 1/2 teaspoons kosher salt

1 1/2 teaspoons ground pepper

1/2 cup olive oil

2 1/2 tablespoons soy oil

Yield: 4 servings

Rigatoni Florentina

If garlic-basil rigatoni is unavailable, choose another garlic-flavored pasta and add basil to the sauce.

12 ounces uncooked
garlic-basil rigatoni
½ to 1 bunch green
onions, sliced
½ to 1 eggplant, chopped
(optional)
1 (4-ounce) can sliced black
olives (optional)
4 cups sliced fresh mushrooms
¼ cup olive oil
12 ounces Italian sausage,
cooked, drained
3 cups prepared chunky garlic
tomato and herb sauce
or other marinara sauce
3 cups shredded mozzarella
cheese
1½ cups grated Parmesan
cheese

Yield: 10 servings

Preheat the oven to 375 degrees.

Cook the pasta in boiling water to cover in a saucepan for 6 to 8 minutes; drain. Let stand until cool.

Sauté the green onions, eggplant, olives and mushrooms in olive oil in a skillet; drain well.

Combine the pasta, sautéed vegetables, Italian sausage and marinara sauce in a medium bowl; mix well.

Layer the pasta mixture, the mozzarella cheese and the Parmesan cheese one half at a time in a baking dish. Bake at 375 degrees for 20 to 25 minutes or until bubbly.

Make this dish ahead of time so the flavors have more time to blend.

Rigatoni with Tomatoes and Vodka

A wonderful, creamy tomato sauce.

Melt the butter in a medium skillet over low heat. Add the onion, garlic and Italian seasoning. Sauté for 3 minutes or until the onion is translucent. Chop the tomatoes, reserving the juice. Add the tomatoes and juice to the onion mixture, stirring gently.

Add the ham. Simmer for 10 minutes. Stir in the vodka. Simmer for 5 minutes longer. Add the whipping cream and ½ cup of the Parmesan cheese. Simmer for 4 minutes or until the sauce is thickened, stirring constantly.

Fold in the pasta, stirring until well coated. Season with white pepper; top with the remaining Parmesan cheese.

2 tablespoons butter
1 small onion, chopped
2 cloves of garlic, minced
1 tablespoon dried Italian
  seasoning
1 (16-ounce) can Italian plum
  tomatoes
3 ounces sliced ham or
  prosciutto, chopped
½ cup vodka
¾ cup whipping cream
1 cup grated Parmesan cheese
8 ounces rigatoni, cooked,
  drained
White pepper to taste

Yield: 4 servings

Warm Asian Beef and Pasta

his Alabama beef award winner has an intriguing blend of flavors. Fresh cilantro or parsley is a must.

1 pound choice boneless top
sirloin, cut ½ inch thick
1 tablespoon olive oil
1 teaspoon garlic powder
¼ cup crunchy peanut butter
¼ cup soy sauce
2 tablespoons dark sesame oil
¼ cup rice wine vinegar
2 teaspoons sugar
2 tablespoons water
¼ teaspoon pepper
4 large green onions, sliced
into 1-inch sections
4 cups hot cooked spaghetti,
drained
1 tablespoon sesame seeds,
toasted
2 tablespoons chopped fresh
cilantro or parsley
Red bell pepper strips

Yield: 4 servings

Slice the beef crosswise into ⅛-x2-inch strips.

Heat the olive oil in a medium skillet; add the beef strips and ½ teaspoon of the garlic powder. Stir-fry for 5 minutes or until of the desired degree of doneness. Remove from the heat and keep warm.

Whisk the remaining ½ teaspoon garlic powder, peanut butter, soy sauce, sesame oil, rice wine vinegar, sugar, water and pepper in a large bowl. Stir in the green onions.

Place the hot pasta in a large bowl. Add the beef and dressing mixture, tossing to combine. Spoon onto a serving platter. Top with the toasted sesame seeds and cilantro.

Garnish with red bell pepper strips.

Iron Fence at Train Depot

Chip Cooper

The romance of travel by train is almost palpable at the Huntsville Depot Museum. The first train arrived in Huntsville in 1855 when the Memphis and Charleston Railroad completed tracks into Huntsville. Completed in 1860, the Depot is one of America's oldest surviving railroad buildings.

Photograph right:
Raspberry Roulage
Lemon Butter Tarts
Crème de Menthe Pie

Overleaf:
German Sand Torte

Desserts

❧

The wall was damp and mossy
when we crossed the street
and said we loved the south . . .
and I thought I was part
of the south. . . . The wistaria
along the fence was green
and the shade was cool
and life was old.

—Zelda Fitzgerald
The Collected Writings

Coffee Meringues with Butterscotch Mousse

You'll want to eat these tasty coffee meringues even without the filling.

Preheat the oven to 225 degrees.

Cut 2 sheets of heavy non-recycled brown paper the size of a baking sheet and place on 2 nonstick baking sheets.

Combine the egg whites, coffee granules and cream of tartar in a medium bowl; beat until the mixture is foamy. Add the sugar 1 tablespoon at a time, beating until stiff.

Drop by rounded teaspoonfuls onto the prepared baking sheets. Bake at 225 degrees for 1¼ hours. Turn off the oven. Let the meringues stand in the closed oven for 2 hours or longer.

Remove the meringues carefully from the brown paper. Store in an airtight container for up to 1 week. Spoon Butterscotch Mousse onto each meringue just before serving. Garnish with chocolate-covered coffee beans.

Butterscotch Mousse

Combine the butterscotch chips, butter, coffee granules and water in a heavy saucepan. Cook over low heat until the chips and butter are melted, stirring constantly.

Stir about one fourth of the hot mixture gradually into the beaten egg in a small bowl; stir the egg mixture into the hot mixture. Cook for 1 minute longer. Remove from heat. Let stand until cooled to room temperature.

Fold the whipped cream gently into the cooled mixture. Chill for 8 to 12 hours.

3 egg whites
1 teaspoon instant coffee granules
¼ teaspoon cream of tartar
1 cup sugar

Butterscotch Mousse
1 cup butterscotch chips
3 tablespoons butter
1 tablespoon instant coffee granules
3 tablespoons water
1 egg, lightly beaten
1 cup whipping cream, whipped

Yield: 50 meringues

Praline Cheesecake

*P*raline topping makes this the quintessential
Southern cheesecake.

1 cup graham cracker crumbs

¼ cup (about) melted butter

24 ounces cream cheese,
softened

1¼ cups packed brown sugar

3 eggs

2 tablespoons flour

1 teaspoon vanilla extract

¼ cup butter, softened

½ cup packed brown sugar

Yield: 12 servings

Preheat the oven to 350 degrees.

Combine graham cracker crumbs with enough butter to hold crumbs together. Press the mixture firmly into a 9-inch springform pan. Set aside.

Beat the cream cheese and 1¼ cups brown sugar in a large bowl. Add the eggs 1 at a time, beating well after each addition. Add the flour and vanilla; mix well.

Pour into the prepared pan.

Bake at 350 degrees for 45 minutes. Let stand until cool.

Melt ¼ cup butter in a small saucepan over low heat. Add ½ cup brown sugar; mix well. Pour over the cooled cheesecake.

Chill until serving time.

Sherried Peaches with Ice Cream

A stunning choice for a special summertime occasion. Buy the best vanilla ice cream to serve with these succulent peaches when you don't have time to make your own.

Whisk the egg yolks, confectioners' sugar and kirsch in a large bowl until light and fluffy. Whisk in 1 or 2 drops of vanilla. Fold the whipping cream into the egg mixture.

Divide the mixture among 4 small freezerproof molds. Freeze, covered, for 2 hours.

Chill 4 individual dessert plates for the ice cream.

Poach 2 whole peaches with the orange slices in a mixture of the sauterne, ½ cup sugar and several drops of vanilla in a medium saucepan for 10 minutes. Let cool in the syrup. Drain, reserving the syrup.

Peel and slice the remaining 3 peaches.

Caramelize the remaining ½ cup sugar in a small heavy-bottomed saucepan over low heat, stirring constantly. Remove from the heat and stir in the reserved syrup. Cook over low heat until all the sugar has dissolved, stirring constantly.

Add the sliced peaches and peach brandy. Simmer for 10 minutes, stirring occasionally. Press the sliced peaches through a sieve into a bowl. Add orange juice and sugar to taste. Peel the poached peaches, cut into halves and remove the pits.

Unmold the ice cream onto the 4 chilled dessert plates. Cut each ice cream mold into halves, and ease the 2 halves apart. Spoon the peach brandy sauce around the ice cream. Place a poached peach half on top. Garnish the edge of the plate with whipped cream and dots of grenadine.

6 egg yolks

¾ cup confectioners' sugar

¼ cup kirsch

1 or 2 drops of vanilla extract

2¼ cups whipping cream

5 peaches

2 orange slices, peel and
   membranes removed

2¼ cups sherry

½ cup sugar

Vanilla extract to taste

½ cup sugar

¼ teaspoon peach brandy

Juice of ½ orange

Sugar to taste

Yield: 4 servings

Pears Poached in Red Wine

his elegant, enticing dessert is featured on our cover.

4 whole large ripe pears
with stems
3 tablespoons lemon juice
3 cups dry red wine
⅓ cup sugar
1 teaspoon vanilla extract
1 cinnamon stick
2 tablespoons brandy
4 scoops French vanilla
ice cream

Yield: 4 servings

Peel the pears, leaving the stems intact. Scoop out the cores from the bottom. Combine with 2 tablespoons lemon juice and enough water to cover in a bowl. Set aside.

Bring the wine to a simmer in a saucepan large enough to hold the pears upright. Add the sugar, vanilla and cinnamon stick. Heat until the sugar dissolves. Add the pears. Cook over low heat for 15 minutes or until tender but still firm.

Remove the pears from the saucepan; drain and place in a shallow dish.

Bring the wine mixture to a boil. Cook rapidly until the liquid is reduced to ¾ cup and is syrupy. Add remaining 1 tablespoon lemon juice and the brandy. Spoon the syrup over the pears. Cool to room temperature or chill, basting occasionally with the syrup.

Place 1 scoop of the ice cream into each of 4 stemmed serving dishes. Cut the pears into quarters from the bottoms almost to the tops. Spread the pear quarters open slightly and arrange stem side up over the ice cream. Garnish with fresh mint or fresh raspberries.

Grilled Pineapple with Kirsch

*K*irsch, a white brandy made of cherries, adds a delightfully unexpected touch to this dramatic dessert.

Slice the pineapple into halves vertically, slicing through the leaves. Cut the rind off the end of each half so that it can stand upright. Slice each half into thirds vertically, slicing through the leaves and keeping them attached.

Cut and discard the tough central core that runs the length of each section. Cut the flesh away from the rind at the bottom using a sharp knife, keeping the flesh in a single piece for each section and leaving as little of it attached to the rind as possible.

Cut the pineapple flesh crosswise to make ½- to ¾-inch-thick slices. Shift slices alternately to the left and to the right for a decorative effect.

Preheat the grill. Wrap the leaves of each section in foil and arrange the pineapple on the grill. Sprinkle with sugar. Grill for 8 minutes or until light brown. Remove foil and sprinkle with kirsch. Serve immediately.

Note: Pineapple may be broiled instead of grilled.

1 large pineapple with an attractive crown of leaves
1½ tablespoons sugar
2 tablespoons kirsch

Yield: 6 servings

Southern Peach Cake

A family favorite for generations. The heavenly aroma that fills your kitchen will remind you of visits to grandmother's house.

½ cup butter, melted

1 cup sugar

2 eggs, beaten

2 tablespoons milk

1½ cups flour

1½ teaspoons baking powder

¾ cup sugar

2 teaspoons flour

¾ teaspoon cinnamon

3 cups sliced peaches

Yield: 15 servings

Preheat the oven to 350 degrees.

Beat the butter, sugar and eggs in a medium bowl until well blended. Add the milk; blend well. Add 1½ cups flour mixed with baking powder; mix well.

Pour into a greased 9x13-inch cake pan.

Combine ¾ cup sugar, 2 teaspoons flour and cinnamon in a small bowl. Sprinkle half the mixture over the batter. Sprinkle peaches with the remaining cinnamon mixture. Arrange peach slices on top.

Bake at 350 degrees for 45 to 50 minutes or until the cake tests done.

Serve warm with whipped topping or ice cream.

White Chocolate Cake

A wonderful cake in the grand tradition of Southern cake baking. Serve it at Christmastime garnished with chocolate holly leaves and fresh raspberries.

Preheat the oven to 350 degrees.

Combine the white chocolate and boiling water in a small saucepan, stirring until the white chocolate is melted; set aside.

Cream the margarine and sugar in a large bowl until light and fluffy. Add the egg yolks 1 at a time, mixing well after each addition. Add the melted white chocolate and vanilla; mix well.

Sift the flour, baking soda and salt together. Add the sifted dry ingredients to the creamed mixture alternately with the buttermilk, mixing well after each addition. Beat the egg whites in a small bowl until stiff peaks form. Fold the egg whites gently into the white chocolate mixture.

Pour the batter into three 9-inch layer cake pans lined with waxed paper.

Bake at 350 degrees for 30 to 40 minutes or until the cake tests done. Cool in pans for 10 minutes. Remove to wire racks to cool completely.

Spread the warm White Chocolate Icing between the layers and over the top, allowing icing to drizzle down the sides.

White Chocolate Icing

Combine the white chocolate, salt, confectioners' sugar and hot water in a medium bowl; beat until blended. Add the margarine 2 tablespoons at a time, beating well after each addition. Beat in the egg yolks. Stir in the vanilla.

4 ounces white chocolate

½ cup boiling water

1 cup margarine, softened

2 cups sugar

4 egg yolks

1 teaspoon vanilla extract

2½ cups flour

½ teaspoon baking soda

½ teaspoon salt

1 cup buttermilk

4 egg whites

White Chocolate Icing

12 ounces white chocolate, melted

Dash of salt

1½ cups confectioners' sugar

¼ cup hot water

¼ cup margarine, softened

2 egg yolks, beaten

1 teaspoon vanilla extract

Yield: 16 servings

Raspberry Roulage

If you've never tried to make a roulage, this beautiful dessert is your reason to learn. Even if it does tear a bit, it will still be delicious.

1 cup semi-sweet chocolate

3 tablespoons hot water

5 egg yolks, beaten

¾ cup sugar

1 teaspoon vanilla extract

5 egg whites

Baking cocoa

½ cup seedless raspberry jam

2 tablespoons framboise

3 cups whipping cream

¼ cup sugar

Raspberry Sauce

4 cups fresh raspberries

1 cup sugar or to taste

3 to 4 tablespoons freshly squeezed lemon juice

Yield: 12 servings

Preheat the oven to 300 degrees.

Combine the chocolate with hot water in a double boiler. Heat until chocolate melts.

Beat the egg yolks with the sugar. Stir in the melted chocolate and the vanilla. Beat the egg whites until stiff peaks form. Fold gently into the chocolate mixture. Spoon the mixture into a 10x15-inch jelly roll pan lined with buttered waxed paper.

Bake at 300 degrees for 20 to 25 minutes or until the cake tests done. Remove the pan from the oven. Place a damp cloth over the cake. Let stand for 5 minutes. Sprinkle a length of foil generously with baking cocoa. Invert the cake onto the foil. Score the cake about every inch; do not cut through the cake. Scoring will aid in rolling the cake.

Blend the raspberry jam and the framboise in a small bowl. Spread a thin layer over the cake to the edges. Whip the whipping cream with ¼ cup sugar in a mixer bowl until soft peaks form. Spread the whipped cream over the jam. Roll as for jelly roll. Wrap the cake tightly in foil. Chill for 8 hours. Serve with Raspberry Sauce.

Raspberry Sauce

Purée the raspberries, half the sugar and 3 tablespoons lemon juice in a food processor for 2 to 3 minutes or until the sugar is completely dissolved. Add the remaining sugar by spoonfuls and the remaining lemon juice by drops, if needed, processing constantly. Strain through a sieve into a bowl. Chill, covered, in the refrigerator.

German Sand Torte

The German influence on Huntsville's heritage has found its way into our kitchens. This lovely cake is one example.

Preheat the oven to 325 degrees.

Beat the butter in a medium bowl. Beat the eggs in a large bowl until foamy. Mix a small amount of flour with the baking powder; set aside. Combine the remaining flour with the cornstarch.

Add the sugar, butter and flour mixture alternately to the eggs, beating at medium speed after each addition until well blended. Add the rum, lemon zest and baking powder mixture; mix well. Pour into a greased and floured 10-inch tube pan.

Bake at 325 degrees for 1¼ hours or until a wooden pick inserted in the center comes out clean.

Cool in the pan for 10 minutes. Invert onto a cake plate. Let stand until cool.

2 cups butter, softened
8 eggs, at room temperature
2 cups flour, sifted
1 teaspoon baking powder
2 cups cornstarch
4 cups sugar
2 tablespoons rum
Zest of 1 lemon

Yield: 16 servings

Cappuccino Brownies

Proof positive that simple pleasures are the best.

2 pounds milk chocolate chips
or chopped milk chocolate
¼ cup instant coffee granules
1 cup unsalted butter,
softened
2 cups sugar
8 eggs
3 tablespoons vanilla extract
1 teaspoon cinnamon
1 teaspoon salt
2 cups flour

Yield: 6½ dozen

Preheat the oven to 375 degrees.

Place the chocolate chips and the coffee granules in a double boiler over simmering water. Cook over medium heat until the chocolate melts, stirring occasionally.

Beat the butter in a bowl until fluffy. Add the sugar gradually, beating constantly and scraping sides of bowl as necessary. Beat in the eggs 2 at a time. Beat for 3 minutes or until the mixture is pale yellow.

Add the vanilla, cinnamon and salt and mix well. Beat in the chocolate mixture until combined. Beat in the flour until smooth and creamy. Spoon the batter into 4 lightly greased and floured 8-inch square baking pans.

Bake at 375 degrees for 35 minutes or until the edges pull from sides of the pans. Cool on a wire rack. Chill, covered, for 8 to 12 hours. Cut the cold brownies into bars to serve.

Angel Pie

Fill the delicious meringue crust with your choice of lemon or chocolate fillings—or make one of each.

Meringue Shell

Preheat the oven to 325 degrees.

Combine the egg whites and cream of tartar in a bowl and beat until soft peaks form. Add the sugar 1 tablespoon at a time, beating until stiff peaks form. Stir in the vanilla and fold in the pecans. Spoon into a buttered pie plate, pressing to line the bottom and side.

Bake at 325 degrees for 25 minutes or until light brown. Turn off the oven; let stand in closed oven for 8 to 12 hours.

Lemon Filling

Combine the egg yolks, sugar, lemon juice and lemon rind in a double boiler. Cook over hot water until very thick. Cover and let cool.

Spread half the whipped cream in the meringue shell. Stir the filling and layer it over the whipped cream. Spread the remaining whipped cream on top.

Chill, covered, for several hours.

Chocolate Filling

Melt the chocolate with water and salt in a saucepan over low heat, mixing until well blended. Remove from heat. Cool until thickened. Fold in the whipped cream gently. Spoon into the meringue shell.

Chill in the refrigerator. Serve with a generous dollop of whipped cream. Garnish with chocolate curls.

Meringue Shell

3 egg whites

¼ teaspoon cream of tartar

1 cup sugar

1 teaspoon vanilla extract

1 cup pecans, chopped

Lemon Filling

4 egg yolks

½ cup sugar

2 tablespoons lemon juice

1 teaspoon grated lemon rind

1 cup whipping cream,
    whipped

Chocolate Filling

8 ounces German's sweet
    chocolate

3 tablespoons water

¼ teaspoon salt

1 cup whipping cream,
    whipped

Yield: 8 servings

Crème de Menthe Pie

*M*int lovers will be delighted with this recipe. *Garnish with shaved chocolate.*

1¼ cups crushed
Oreo cookies
⅓ cup melted butter
24 large marshmallows
⅔ cup milk, scalded
2 ounces crème de menthe
1 ounce crème de cacao
1 cup whipping cream,
whipped

Yield: 8 servings

Combine the cookie crumbs and butter in a bowl. Pat into a 9-inch pie plate. Chill until firm.

Add the marshmallows to the scalded milk in a double boiler. Cook over hot water until the marshmallows melt, stirring frequently. Cool to room temperature.

Add the crème de menthe and the crème de cacao. Fold in the whipped cream gently. Pour into the crust. Freeze, covered, for 2 hours or longer. Thaw slightly before serving.

May be made up to a month ahead and frozen until ready to use.

Frozen Strawberry Margarita Pie

This cool, refreshing dessert is a slice of paradise after a hot and spicy meal.

Combine the pretzel crumbs, margarine and sugar in a bowl; mix lightly. Press firmly over the bottom and up the side of a lightly buttered 10-inch pie plate.

Combine the condensed milk, strawberries, lime juice, tequila, Triple Sec and food coloring in a large bowl; mix well. Fold in the whipped cream. Pour into the crust.

Freeze for 4 hours or until firm. Let stand at room temperature for 10 minutes before serving.

Note: Substitute frozen unsweetened strawberries, thawed and drained, for the fresh strawberries if desired.

1¼ cups finely crushed pretzels

½ cup plus 2 tablespoons margarine, melted

¼ cup sugar

1 (14-ounce) can sweetened condensed milk

1½ cups chopped fresh strawberries

⅓ cup lime juice

¼ cup tequila

2 tablespoons Triple Sec

3 drops of red food coloring (optional)

1½ cups whipping cream, whipped

Yield: 10 servings

Skillet Apple Tart with Calvados Cream

*T*his traditional French upside-down tart
has the special Southern twist of being baked in
a cast-iron skillet. The apples caramelize on
the bottom of the skillet. When inverted,
the tantalizing apples crown the tart.

5 Golden Delicious apples

1½ cups sugar

4 cups water

1 cinnamon stick

Zest of 1 lemon, grated

6 whole cloves

½ vanilla bean

¾ cup sugar

2 tablespoons unsalted butter

1 tablespoon lemon juice

1 teaspoon freshly
grated nutmeg

2 tablespoons Calvados

½ package puff pastry sheets

Calvados Cream

1 cup whipping cream

1 tablespoon sugar

2 to 3 tablespoons Calvados

Yield: 8 servings

Peel, halve and core the apples. Combine 1½ cups sugar, water, cinnamon stick, lemon zest, cloves and vanilla bean in a large saucepan. Simmer for 10 minutes.

Add the apples. Simmer for 5 to 10 minutes or just until barely tender; remove the apples while still firm. Drain and cool.

Place ¾ cup sugar in a 10-inch cast-iron skillet. Cook over medium heat until the sugar syrup turns golden brown, stirring carefully. Remove to a cool surface. Center 1 apple half in the skillet. Arrange 6 halves around the center. Slice the remaining 3 halves; place over the top to fill in the spaces.

Preheat the oven to 425 degrees.

Melt the butter in a saucepan. Add the lemon juice, nutmeg and 2 tablespoons Calvados; mix well. Drizzle the mixture over the apples. Cut an 11-inch circle from the puff pastry sheet. Place over the top of the apples.

Bake at 425 degrees for 30 to 35 minutes or until the pastry is deep brown and puffed. Cool for 15 minutes. Invert the skillet onto a serving platter.

Serve warm or at room temperature with Calvados Cream or whipped cream.

Calvados Cream

Combine the whipping cream, sugar and Calvados in a chilled bowl. Whip very lightly or just until thickened.

Lemon Butter Tarts

arnish the Lemon Butter Tarts with fresh strawberries or sugared mint leaves.

Tart Shells

Sift the flour and salt into a bowl and mix well. Add the butter and cold water; mix quickly until the dough forms a ball. Divide into 2 equal portions and press flat. Wrap the dough in waxed paper. Chill for 1 hour or until firm.

Preheat the oven to 350 degrees. Roll out each portion of the dough with a floured rolling pin on a floured surface. Cut to fit 2 tart pans. Trim and flute edge. Prick the bottom of each shell with a fork.

Bake at 350 degrees until lightly browned. Cool on a wire rack. Store, tightly wrapped, in the freezer.

Lemon Butter Tarts

Beat the eggs and egg yolks in a bowl. Combine with the sugar in a double boiler. Add the lemon rind, lemon juice and butter; mix well.

Cook over simmering water over low heat until of custard consistency, stirring constantly. Cool. Spoon into baked Tart Shells to serve. Store in the refrigerator.

Tart Shells
2½ cups flour
Pinch of salt
¾ cup butter, melted, cooled
6 tablespoons cold water

Lemon Butter Tarts
6 eggs
2 egg yolks
2 cups sugar
Grated rind of 1 lemon
Juice of 4 lemons
1 cup butter

Yield: 12 servings

Acknowledgments

The Junior League of Huntsville gratefully acknowledges the following supporters of *Sweet Home Alabama* for their many and varied contributions.

Alabama Constitution Village
Dr. and Mrs. Gilbert A. Aust
Mr. and Mrs. Philip Bentley, III
Mr. and Mrs. E. Wayne Bonner
Mr. and Mrs. Greg V. Bragg
Brooks & Collier
Burritt Museum and Park
Bubs Owen Calloway
Mr. and Mrs. Kit Carlton
Dr. and Mrs. Gordon C. Cash
Ceramic Harmony
Mr. and Mrs. Henry H. Chase
City of Huntsville
Susan Berry Clanton
Beverly Boerner Farrington
James A. Fleming
Dr. and Mrs. Carl J. Gessler, Jr.
Betty Wallenborn Green
Mr. and Mrs. William H. Gray
Green Bottle Grill
Mr. and Mrs. Charles F. Grisham
Hampton Cove
Harrison Brothers
Dr. and Mrs. John T. Hartley
Mrs. William G. Henson
Mr. and Mrs. John R. Howard
Huntsville Botanical Garden
Huntsville Stars
Huntsville Train Depot
Dr. Eleanor Newman Hutchens
Intergraph
Dr. John Rison Jones

Mr. and Mrs. Jeff E. Kaufmann
Mr. and Mrs. Mike Kelly
Mr. and Mrs. Thompson R. Kelly
Mr. and Mrs. George King
Lawren's
Mr. and Mrs. Peter L. Lowe
Mrs. Frederick H. Martin
Mr. and Mrs. Jim Martin
Nell Lipscomb Martin
Mr. and Mrs. James R. McCown
Mr. and Mrs. D. Scott McLain
Mr. and Mrs. William T. O'Meara
Jean Harper Payne
Mr. and Mrs. Ronald W. Pidgeon
Mr. and Mrs. William S. Propst
Mr. and Mrs. Michael K. Reiney
Dr. and Mrs. Marshall T. Schreeder
Mr. and Mrs. Vernon G. Schrimsher
Lee Sentell
John M. Shaver
Charles E. Shaver, III
Mr. and Mrs. Jeff W. Sikes
Mr. and Mrs. Claude E. Sparks
Mr. and Mrs. Ralph G. Stubblefield, Jr.
Mr. and Mrs. Eloy Torrez
U. S. Space & Rocket Center
Mr. and Mrs. Harold M. Vandervoort
Mr. and Mrs. Ray F. Vandiver, Jr.
Mrs. Ruth von Saurma
Weeden House Museum
Dr. and Mrs. Don A. Wheeler
Mr. and Mrs. Danny L. Wiginton

Chip Cooper

*Photographer Chip Cooper is a Southern visionary described as one who uses the painter's eye to evoke his camera images. His photography has captured the Alabama landscape in the renowned **Alabama Memories;** his regional **Silent in the Land** is described by author Harper Lee as "a visual feast." Featured in magazines throughout the country, he has provided the photography for several books and has participated in various one-man and group exhibits. An adjunct professor in the Department of Art-Photography and Director of Photography at the University of Alabama, he has won numerous awards and honors, including Communication Arts Magazine's Award of Excellence, Book Series 1994. His photographs are held in many private corporate and museum collections.*

Bridge with Cherry Trees

Chip Cooper

*The Oriental bridge in Big Spring Park, a gift from Japanese
Major General Mikio Kimata, once stationed at Redstone Arsenal,
is a fitting symbol of Huntsville's international flavor. Huntsville's
founders were attracted to the Big Spring, which, with the adjacent
von Braun Civic Center, still forms the cultural heart of the city.*

Sweet Home Alabama Committee

Chairman
Debbie Rice Kaufmann

Co-Chairman
Sarah Faulkner Kelly

Co-Chairman
Mary Lynn Vandiver Carlton

Production Chairman
Joia Johnson Thompson

Food Editor
Carole Jurenko Jones

Photography Coordinator
Caroline Kelly

Photography Stylists
Mary Lynn Vandiver Carlton
Janna Schrimsher Martin

Writers/Editors
Kim Sherman Hartley
Lucinda Martin Schreeder
René Boom Stubblefield

Finance Chairman
Karen Goodwin Smith

Marketing Chairman
Jennifer Bond Cash

Special Events Coordinators
Lisa Cox Edwards
Pam Noller Moores
René Boom Stubblefield

Sustainer Advisors
Trisha Finlen Bragg
Elise Kuh Goodson
June Howard Guynes
Ann White Hay
Sheila Turner-Torrez
Martha McCown Vandiver

**League Presidents
(1991-1995)**
Lucinda Martin Schreeder
Trisha Finlen Bragg
Cynthia Bagby Richardson
Beth Holliman McLain
Kim Sherman Hartley

Section Editors
Joy McGlynn Belmont
Sallie Lankford Ennis
Leila Culver Hergert
Nita Arrington Maddox
Jean Ann Wilson Maples
Cindy Kirkland Randall
Barbara Ann Ross
Lee Cattlett Seeley

Marketing Committee
Lora Shuey Abernathy
Joy McGlynn Belmont
Pam Jones Cash
Beth Langford Chenowith
Amy Moore Christopher
Marie McGown Coyne
Lynne Lassiter Duncan
Lisa Copeland Earles
Sallie Lankford Ennis
Amy Sparks Epps
Betsy Freshney Estopinal
Leila Culver Hergert
Susan Ross Hoyle
Faye Lind Jenson
Pennie Shihadeh Keene
Donna Brooks Lehman
Lori Brown Lester
Julie Huettel Lowe
Leigh Anne Pettis Luther
Nita Arrington Maddox
Kelly Hargrove Markwalter
Missy Maxwell
Kim Park Mims
Margaret Strawn Morring
Cindy Kirkland Randall
Barbara Ann Ross
Lee Cattlett Seeley
Erica Valentino Smith
Rebecca Horne Sterling
Kelley Golden Zelickson

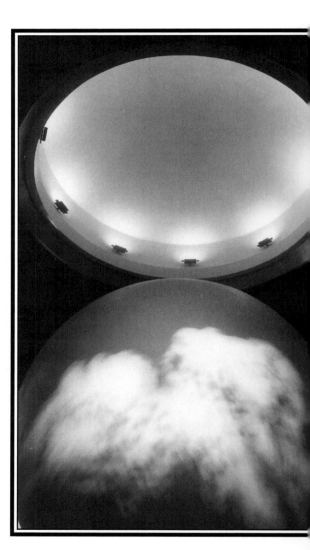

Illuminated Sphere   Chip Cooper

Mysteriously illuminated, the sphere representing the planet Earth glows in the center of the main exhibit hall of the Center for Biospheric Education and Research at the Huntsville/Madison County Botanical Garden. The Garden features the pastoral beauty of a traditional botanical garden with an emphasis on preserving the Earth's delicate biosphere.

Recipe Contributors

Lora Shuey Abernathy
Lisa Hunter Adair
Mary Gamble Adams
Eloise Lundberg Alexander
Laurie Allen
Lowry Spraggins Allen
Patty Atherton
Mae Awbury
Beth Camp Babin
Ramona Baker
Sara Landers Baker
Joann Vayda Bee
Joy McGlynn Belmont
Scott Berg
Jean Millsaps Berry
Leigh Morrow Birchfield
Brenda Hill Black
Dot Boerner
Pete Boscio
Allison Bowden
Chris Burson Bragg
Glenda Vann Bragg
Trisha Finlen Bragg
Monica Chien Brindley
Mary Alice Kelly Brinkley
Melissa Crute Brinkley
Kakki Jordan Brooks
Jeanne Holmes Brown
Teena Earley Brown
Flora Brunson
Pam Schrimsher Buck
Faith Couvillon Bunn
Elaine Churchill Calhoun
Bubs Owen Callaway
Mary Lynn Vandiver Carlton
Kedra Carriger
Tammy Stover Caruso
Jennifer Bond Cash
Myrna Humm Cattlett
Marion Snow Certain
Barbara Chappell
Laura Lively Charlton
Venette Cox Charlton
Bev Sabol Chase
Nancy Chase
Susan Berry Clanton
Pattie Johnston Cline
North River Yacht Club
Jeannie Bennett Cole
Alleda Whatley Coons
Mabel Corbett
Ann Carter Corley
Cheryl Couch
Laura Brown Cragon
Dawn Crouch
Winifred Murphree Crute
Karen Cruz
Sally Ann Palmerlee Culver
Willadean Curry
Rebecca Jones Curtis
Butch Kohler Damson
Claudia Looney Davis
Jeanette Davis

Mary Beth Flynn Davis
Susan Mayes Davis
Teen Deroode
Kate McDonnell Downing
Cindy Durst
Lisa Cox Edwards
Mary Berry England
Sallie Lankford Ennis
Amy Sparks Epps
Donna Smith Epps
Betsy Freshney Estopinal
Lynne Sadler Evans
Adie Evans Fann
Beverly Boerner Farrington
Virginia Harper Faulkner
Denise Ann Ferguson
Bitsy Thomas Flake
Pam Fleming
Lila Pryor Frank
William Gantt
Jill Abernathy Gardner
Stacey Strickland Gardner
Jan Quarles Garrett
Thalia Garrison
Andi Holiman Gaskins
Thalia Crone Gaskins
Ellen Gentle
Sarah Westbrook Gessler
Anne Owen Golden
Elise Kuh Goodson
Emily Elise Goodson
Pat Goodson
Jeri Gore
Christine Young Grice
Linda Condra Griffin
June Howard Guynes
Aileen Halcomb
Dan Halcomb
Karen Kimbrell Hall
Jewel Fernandez Halsey
Willa Ham
Laura Jo Hamilton
Harvilee Phillips Harbarger
Linda Hargrove
Doni Tucker Harrison
Joan Hopkins Harrison
Kim Sherman Hartley
Patsy Binkley Haws
Adalene Kelly Hay
Ann White Hay
Kathryn Hearn
Carol Bevels Hedden
Leila Culver Hergert
Liz Byers Herrin
Buena Hester
Ruth Hicks
Terry Hodge
Jeanett Honeycutt
Grace Hooper
Cora Lee Horne
Joyce Horne
Mary Ann Daniel Howell
Bobsy Gaskins Ingram

Mae Belle Jackson
Belle Jennings
Kelley Johns
Nan Johnson
Sydna Wells Johnson
Carole Jurenko Jones
Judy Jones
Ruth Jurenko
Debbie Rice Kaufmann
Mae Kavanaugh
Pennie Shihadeh Keene
Caroline Kelly
Cathy Hay Kelly
Dotty Jones Kelly
Nancy Hall Kelly
Sarah Faulkner Kelly
Robbie Kimbrough
Carla Miller King
Shelbie King
Claudia Hopkins Klus
Jan Krell
Trish Landwehr
Janis Langley
Betty Lankford
Martha Lankford
Miriam Lau
Robin Gillespie Leberte
Debbie Lewis
Lynn Hay Littrell
Phyllis Lively
Karen Lovell
Lynne Berry Lowery
Kathy Lansdell Ludwig
Nita Arrington Maddox
Julie Meigs Malone
Covey McKee Maples
Jean Ann Wilson Maples
Stuart M. Maples
Jana Schrimser Martin
Vivian Fleming Martin
Sarabeth Martinson
Mrs. S. L. Mathison
Jane Alford McBride
Betty Hutchens McCaleb
Jeanne Luther McCown
Eugenia Elebash McCoy
Sue Coons McDaniel
Betty McGlynn
Beth Holliman McLain
Jan Price McMurray
Mary McVay
Barbara Kelso McWilliams
Suzie Crowe Mickle
Carolyn Miles
Elizabeth Dembo Miller
Mary Elizabeth Mills
Jane Cain Monroe
Emily Word Moody
Virginia Moon
Beth Price Moore
Pam Noller Moores
Susan Tuggle Moquin
Anne Morard

Lilie Hill
Margaret Strawn Morring
Marilyn Jones Morring
Martha Phillips Morring
Mike Morring
Pamela Thrash Morring
Sandy Morring
Sarah Mullins
Jeannie Guerin Munger
Melanie Murray
Minnie Lois Yarbrough Neal
Kay Newton
Mindy Niedermeyer
Laurie Kuppersmith Noojin
Cindy Bogard O'Gorman
Jane Odle
Wynn Hamilton Oldham
Laura Bratcher Page
May Pascal
Lucille Patton
Norvell Patton
Jean Harper Payne
Linda Patterson Pearce
Gloria Terry Pennington
Kathy Sundy Perkins
Mary Kate Perkins
Kathleen Whitfield Perry
Barbara Ross Phillips
Ron Pidgeon
Mildred Pizitz
Anne Cathey Pollard
Susan Alcott Pope
Sandra Simmons Porter
Dolores Pritts
Shirley Riley Pugh
Beth Balch Ragland
Cindy Kirkland Randall
Karen Kelly Reed
Bettie Hopkins Rice
Cathy Williams Rice
Karen Knight Rice
Wendy Ferdinand Rice
Bettye Richardson
Cynthia Bagby Richardson
Nancy McLean Richardson
Lisa Rodgers Roberts
Betsy Gilchrist Robinson
Chris Rodgers
Emily Chase Rodgers
Robert Rodgers
Wynn Payne Rodgers
Suzanne Rogers
Barbara Ann Ross
Sharon Miller Russell
Wade Russell
Camille Morring Salisbury
Marsha Jones Samples
Lucinda Martin Schreeder
Pat Schrimsher
Susan Bragg Schutzenhofer
Ashley King Scoggins
Lee Cattlett Seeley
Paul Seery

Donna Hodges Shergy
Stephanie Sosaya Sherman
Nancy Garth Shotts
Peggy Payne Sington
Cathie Cattlett Smaga
Alyce Palmerlee Smith
Barbara Hunter Smith
Francis Smith
Liz King Smith
Dorothy Goodson Snowden
Peggy Powell Sockwell
Christian C. Sowder
Sally Cox Spencer
Juanita Steele
Julie Harbarger Stephens
Rebecca Horne Sterling
Sue Harris Sterling
Tish Wiggins Stevens
April Richardson Stewart
Sandra Stewart
Ethel Parker Strawn
Jo Stroud
René Boom Stubblefield
Leigh Anne Szukelewicz
Eva Taylor
Alice Kay Thomasson
Iris Vandiver Thorpe
Anne Harris Tincher
Jane Walker Troup
Bill Tucker
Maxine Tuggle
Carlyn Elizabeth Turner
Michael Turner
Lane Malone Tutt
Barbara Uhlich
Sharon Mazza Valavicius
Martha McCown Vandiver
Terrie Brooks Vandiver
Ruth von Saurma
Jean Robinson Walker
Sally Fleming Walker
Steve Wall
Cathy Hunt Ward
Jean Clark Ward
Ashley Watters
Mrs. Lawrence Wear
Peggy Fowler Weaver
Debbie Widgren
Lyn Newcomb Wiginton
Cintra Elgin Willcox
Eloise Williams
Nancy Williams
Gloria Clark Wilson
Elizabeth Machtolff Wise
Wilma Woodard
Beth Young
Betty Young
Kathy Younger
Kelley Golden Zelickson
Green Bottle Grill
Sister Shubert
Vincent's Market

Active and Sustaining Members

Lora Shuey Abernathy
Gay Kelly Abney
Mary Gamble Adams
Eloise Lundberg Alexander
Ann Baugh Allen
Claudia Anderson
Kathleen Cannon Anderson
Dana Block Averbuch
Beth Camp Babin
Nancy Hamilton Bagby
Beth Howard Bailey
Alex Graves Baird
Ann Harper Baker
Linda Austin Baker
Sara Landers Baker
Lee Hill Barber
Edith Chaney Barnett
Mary Ann Blanton Barr
Jane Wright Barran
Tracy Barton
Donna Aliba Basore
Lori Leberte Bates
Eula Sammons Battle
Jane Phillips Battle
Helen Weber Bebb
Paige Ricketts Beitel
Joy McGlynn Belmont
Alice Samples Bentley
Samantha Hereford Bentley
Becky Turnipseed Bergquist
Amanda Priddy Berkey
Kelly Brantley Berryhill
Stephanie C. Billingslea
Jane Boven Bise
Jane Ann Evans Blankenship
Carolyn Jones Blue
Isabel Hill Blue
Lee Watkins Boles
Charlene Puckett Bonner
Ginny Cato Bouldin
Chris Burson Bragg
Glenda Vann Bragg
Laurie Reid Bragg
Trisha Finlen Bragg
Mary Manning Brinkley
Melissa Crute Brinkley
Jane Maxwell Brocato
Sara Miller Brock
Kakki Jordan Brooks
Kim McCary Brooks
Virginia McCulloch Brosemer
Helena Miller Brown
Jeanne Holmes Brown
Linda Williams Brown
Mary Hart Thompson Brown
Teena Earley Brown
Susan Pasierb Browning
Susan Westbrook Bryant
Richlyn Vandiver Buchanan
Faith Couvillon Bunn

Diana Smith Burkett
Robbie Baskin Burlison
Emily Pryor Burwell
Sophia Silver Burwell
Mary Christ Butler
Carol Frantz Byers
Janie Craft Byers
Suzanne Graham Byrom
Rebekah Adams Callahan
Bubs Owen Callaway
Susan Zook Callaway
Lisa Caruso Caprio
Mary Lynn Vandiver Carlton
Edna Crowe Carroll
Tamara Stover Caruso
Virginia Ruebel Caruso
Jennifer Bond Cash
Pam Jones Cash
Carline Stephens Castellow
Helen Wilson Caudle
Marion Snow Certain
Lea Crumpton Chaffin
Janis Chamberlain-Brooks
Libby Adams Chambers
Karen Powell Chandler
Valerie Schild Chandler
Bonnie Klein Chapman
Jeanmarie McGehee Chappell
Sarah Spencer Chappell
Laura Lively Charlton
Venette Cox Charlton
Beverly Sabol Chase
Elizabeth Langford
  Chenoweth
Betty Bell Chesnut
Amy Moore Christopher
Cruse Patton Clark
Bonnie Wright Clemons
Pattie Johnston Cline
Sheila Stinnett Cloud
Susan Cloud
Sallie Kelly Cobb
Ann Gilmore Coffey
Martha Miller Coffman
Jeannie Bennett Cole
Mary Collins
Mitzi McKinney Collins
Ann Pollard Conner
Marion Thorington Conover
Alleda Whatley Coons
Linda Lambert Cope
Susan Morring Cope
Amy Moore Cornelius
Nancy Cowley
Marion Lamar Cox
Marie McGown Coyne
Laura Brown Cragon
Joyce King Crim
Margaret Belle Mahoney
  Crow

Chesley Kelly Crute
Winifred Murphree Crute
Sally Ann Palmerlee Culver
Rebecca Jones Curtis
Butch Kohler Damson
Danielle Day Damson
Louise Jordan Daniel
Stephanie Toomey Daves
Shannon Alexander Davidson
Claudia Looney Davis
Mary Beth Flynn Davis
Susan Mayes Davis
Zoe Powell Davis
Mary Beasley Dean
Donna Satterfield Deaton
Donna Roland DeLisle
Judy Ferris DeRosier
Lynn DeYoung
Lorene Fisk Dilworth
Anna McCulloch Dinwiddie
Bonner Nelson Dison
Lisa Doherty
Vivian Hester Donovan
Layne Bishop Dorning
Kathleen Wells Dotts
Kate McDonnell Downing
Jill Holmes Driscoll
Lynn Lassiter Duncan
Eloise Hightower Dunn
Mary Frances Mahaffie Dunn
Tyler Terry Dyer
Lisa Copeland Earles
Mary Frances Fowler Eddins
Kathleen Dunn Edwards
Lisa Cox Edwards
Mickey Womble Ellis
Rhonda Benson Emerson
Mary Berry England
Sallie Lankford Ennis
Amy Sparks Epps
Donna Smith Epps
Betsy Freshney Estopinal
Frances Godman Evans
Lynne Sadler Evans
Marilyn Horton Evans
Janice Shores Everitt
Christine Stewart Falt
Elizabeth Ann Falt
Anne Moorman Farrell
Beverly Boerner Farrington
Denise Ann Ferguson
Bitsy Thomas Flake
Beth Hearn Fleming
Mary Jane Howell Fleming
Sally Hardigree Fleming
Susie Spragins Fleming
Nancy Young Fortner
Lila Pryor Frank
Sara Ann Hill Frank
Seena Sandburg Furman

Nancy Smith Gaines
Mary Ellen Masters Galloway
Jill Abernathy Gardner
Stacey Strickland Gardner
Andrea Holiman Gaskins
Ellen Gentle
Sarah Westbrook Gessler
Belinda Sloan Gilliam
Catherine Kelly Gilliam
Jeni Whorton Golden
Sheryl Golden
Elise Kuh Goodson
Jill Lanier Grace
Sara James Graves
Mary Key Gray
Betty Wallenborn Green
Linda Lloyd Green
Lori Carlile Gregory
Dibby Jones Griffin
Linda Condra Griffin
Susan Ayers Griffin
Virginia King Griffith
Marilyn Thoele Grundy
Lois Gurvey
June Howard Guynes
Karen Kimbrell Hall
Laura Jo Wilbourn Hamilton
Jane Anderson Hamm
Lisa Bragg Harbarger
Berta Jordan Hargett
Carol Anderson Harless
Janet Irons Harris
Anne Anderson Harrison
Doni Tucker Harrison
Kim Sherman Hartley
Lucinda Hartshorne
Laura Aldridge Hash
Patsy Binkley Haws
Adalene Kelly Hay
Ann White Hay
Judy Byrne Heacock
Mary Ena Heath
Carol Bevels Hedden
Libba Parker Helms
Teri Manning Hennington
Margaret Hutchens Henson
Elizabeth Hereford
Jennifer Huffman Hereford
Leila Culver Hergert
Liz Byers Herrin
Bonnie Pearce Hettinger
Marianne Carlisle Hill
Elizabeth Warren Hoelzer
Bunny Buntin Hovater
Judy Jamison Howard
Susan Ross Hoyle
Virginia Larkin Hughey
Marilyn Elliott Hull
Kathy Hoffman Humphrey
Betsy Savage Hunt

Vannah Grisham Husband
Bobsy Gaskins Ingram
Jan Keebler Ingram
Becky Urbany Irwin
Sarah Hamilton James
Debra Nesbitt Jenkins
Mary Beth Scales Jenkins
Faye Lind Jensen
Anne Cox Jewell
Kelley Johns
Nan Johnson
Synda Roton Johnson
Claire Smith Johnston
Carole Jurenko Jones
Jane Ware Jones
Nancy Jane Swindler Jones
Tobye Moncus Jones
Tracy Shields Jones
Mary Kate Boswell Jordan
Laura Perry Joseph
Mary Ellen Coughlin Judah
Julie Ann Kastanakis
Debbie Rice Kaufmann
Shellye Ford Kaufmann
Pennie Shidadeh Keene
Eleanor Ann Holmberg Keith
Caroline Kelly
Dotty Jones Kelly
Leigh Jordan Kelly
Margaret Ann Watkins Kelly
Nancy Hall Kelly
Sarah Faulkner Kelly
Patsy Knight Kesting
Carla Miller King
Julia Wynn Jones King
Shannon Ledford King
Susan Fulton King
Meg Smith Kingsbury
Allyson Moore Kirkpatrick
Carol Kleiner
Nancy George Kramer
Sally Schreiner Lambert
Prissy Bernard Lampert
Diane Ochs Lanier
Stacy Nicaise Lankford
Betsey Robinson Lanoue
Aline Blair Lary
Sherry Shields Lary
Nannette Stockton Laughlin
Robin Gillespie Leberte
Ruth Owen Lee
Donna Brooks Lehman
Jane Lewter Lehman
Midge Leonard
Lori Brown Lester
Corneila Fitzgerald Lewis
Nita Maddox Lewis
Susan Hereford Lewis
Karen Groves Limperis
Rosemary Williams Little

Laura G. Lively
Katherine Thornton
    Lockridge
Ginger Loder
Barbara Dillon Loflin
Betsy Jones Lowe
Jane Knight Lowe
Jeanne Townes Lowe
Julie Huettel Lowe
Lynne Berry Lowery
Michele Fisher Lucas
Kathy Lansdell Ludwig
Leigh Anne Pettis Luther
Jennifer Coffman Lyons
Linda Bills Maccubbin
Nita Arrington Maddox
Carol Cavaliere Madry
Kathryn Bailey Mahoney
Julia Ann Meigs Malone
Alice Elizabeth Manning
Jean Ann Wilson Maples
Kelli Hargrove Markwalter
Jo Wiggins Marsh
Janna Schrimsher Martin
Jean Wilson Martin
Vivian Fleming Martin
Sarabeth Coleman Martinson
Barbara Lowe Matthews
Suzanne Williams Matthews
Missy Maxwell
Jane Alford McBride
Betty Hutchens McCaleb
Mary Jones McCaleb
Jeanne Luther McCown
Laura Reynolds McCown
Eugenia Elebash McCoy
Beverly Risher McCulloch
Nancy Pate McCurdy
Regina Sanders McDaniel
Sue Coons McDaniel
Jane Denton McDonald
Becky Brigman McDowell
Margery McDuffie
Tracie Lewis McEwen
Lusanne Lilly McKenzie
Beth Holliman McLain
Jan Price McMurray
Suzanne Fleenor McNabb
Jill Hasty McNew
Melanie Martin McRae
Barbara Kelso McWilliams
Amy Sladen Meigs
Jeanne Harris Meigs
Sonja Smith Michael
Kayla Bradford Mickle
Lane Dodd Mickle
Susie Crowe Mickle
Suzette René Mikell
Brenda Carroll Milberger
Genie Haigler Miller

Mary Elizabeth Vinson Mills
Kim Cobern Mims
Gay Hinds Money
Jane Cain Monroe
Cecily Smith Moody
Emily Word Moody
Beth Price Moore
Pam Nollen Moores
Jo Ann Money Moorman
Susan Tuggle Moquin
Beth Wheeler Morring
Margaret Strawn Morring
Marilyn Jones Morring
Martha Phillips Morring
Marion Hill Morrow
Mary Alice Dark Moss
Jeannie Guerin Munger
Mary Coral Weller Murphree
Linda Birchmore Musick
Mary Alice Walker Naylor
Minnie Lois Yarbrough Neal
Janet Meigs Neeley
Ruth Eller Neighbors
Susan Claire Neighbors
Susan Kinzer Neighbors
Caroline Tate Noojin
Laurie Kuppersmith Noojin
Linda Goltz Nunn
Elizabeth Helton Nuwayhid
Margaret Blair O'Brien
Cindy Bogard O'Gorman
Alma Jones O'Neal
Wynn Hamilton Oldham
Mary Beck Osborne
Deborah Mullendore
    Overcash
Anne Golden Owen
Appie Geer Owens
Susan Whaley Ozment
Laura Bratcher Page
Charlotte McEachin Park
Margaret Rodgers Park
Susan Damson Park
Virginia Clark Parnell
Cynthia Massey Parsons
Donna Sanders Pate
Annette Bosley Payne
Jean Harper Payne
Lorene Woods Payne
Noreen Slattery Payne
Linda Patterson Pearce
Ginny Peeler
Gloria Ann Terry Pennington
Darwin Davis Perkins
Kathy Sundy Perkins
Katy Perkins
Kathleen Whitfield Perry
Barbara Ross Phillips
Nancy Foster Pike
Linda Turner Plaxco

Anne Cathey Pollard
Xan Pollard
Margaret Van Dyke Poole
Susan Alcott Pope
Lida Elliott Porter
Sandy Simmons Porter
Martha Falt Priddy
Paige Moss Prozan
Sherry Ann Green Pullen
Tine Wright Purdy
Robin O'Brien Quinlivan
Beth Balch Ragland
Sue Turner Ragland
Martha Simms Rambo
Cindy Kirkland Randall
Britt Locklear Rawson
Daphne Thompson Reed
Sarah Phillips Reed
Andree Reeves
Susan Hamm Rehfeld
Emily Propst Reiney
Laura Cifelli Reynolds
Sara Skelton Rich
Cynthia Bagby Richardson
Nancy McLean Richardson
Kerri Johnson Riley
Ann Machtolff Rivard
Jane Grote Roberts
Lisa Rodgers Roberts
Patsy Kratch Roberts
Sarah Monroe Roberts
Katherine Bagby Robertson
Anne Kerringan Robinson
Ellen Earls Robinson
Virginia Gordon Robinson
Emily Chase Rodgers
Wynn Payne Rodgers
Florrie Pedrick Rose
Barbara Ann Ross
Evey Sirote Rouse
Leila Anne Kidd Rowan
Sue Stubley Rowan
April Warren Russell
Sharon Miller Russell
Judy Savage Ryals
Elizabeth Watts Salmon
Betty Schilds Sam
Dianne Paradise Sammons
Suzie McGilvary Sammons
Carol Ann Cummings
    Samples
Marsha Jones Samples
Shannan League Samples
Myra Monk Sanderson
Charlotte Bentley Schlittler
Lucinda Martin Schreeder
Linda Read Schrimsher
Sherrie Smith Schrimsher
Susan Bragg Schutzenhofer
Ashley King Scoggins

Cindy Johnson Seeley
Lee Cattlett Seeley
Mary Claire Dardis Sefton
Amanda Thrasher Segrest
Katie Walker Shaver
Cynthia Chastain Shepard
Donna Hodges Shergy
Nancy Garth Shotts
Maxine Crabtree Sikes
Kim Simonds Simpson
Peggy Payne Sington
Ginna McDuffie Siniard
Becky Andrews Smedstad
Alyce Palmerlee Smith
Barbara H. Smith
Elizabeth Ann Smith
Erica Valentino Smith
Karen Goodwin Smith
Jeanie Rodgers Snoddy
Carla Jones Snodgrass
Helen Elliott Sockwell
Peggy Powell Sockwell
Karen Gruver Spearing
Evelyn White Spearman
Loretta Purdy Spencer
Sally Martin Cox Spencer
Lynne Breeding Starnes
Carol Epsy Stephens
Julie Harbarger Stephens
Rebecca Horne Sterling
Tish Wiggins Stevens
Virginia Giles Stevens
April Richardson Stewart
Nancey Mitchell Stidger
Flo Underwood Stockton
Suzanne Austin Stockton
Carolyn Phillips Stone
Leesa Hill Stroud
René Boom Stubblefield
Susan Sammons Sullins
Amelia McDonald
    Summerville
Penny Lenoir Sumners
Ann Thrasher Swain
Tammy Swann
Leigh Anne Meland
    Szukelewicz
Mary Elizabeth Tait
Karen Hill Taylor
Lisa Dodson Taylor
Perky Hooker Taylor
Sarah Dilworth Thiemonge
June Thigpen
Suzanne Pettus Thomason
Alice Kay Thomasson
Joia Johnson Thompson
Lorrie Keith Thornton
Patti Bragg Thornton
Dorothy Wright Thrasher
Anne Harris Tincher

Lou Ann Blanton Tindell
Charlotte Pritchard Traylor
Jane Walker Troup
Elizabeth Walthall Tubbs
Anne White Tucker
Sheila Turner-Torrez
Lane Malone Tutt
Tina Tynes
Barbara Uhlich
Betty Hazel Hamilton
    Underwood
Sally Ann Underwood
Sharon Mazza Valavicius
Sandra Gray Vallely
Andrea Tutt Vandervoort
Martha McCown Vandiver
Camille Fleming Vaughan
Beth Thornton Vest
Jeanne McCarty Vojticek
Harriet Dunn Waddell
Jean Robinson Walker
Mary Beth Wedemeyer
    Walker
Mary Katherine Lowry
    Walker
Sally Fleming Walker
Sharon Lazzari Walker
Bess Pratt Wallace
Barbara Byrne Ward
Cathy Hunt Ward
Anna Baker Warren
Jean Cummings Watts
Linda Boyd Watts
Wimberley McLain Watts
Meg Graves Weaver
Peggy Weaver
Lee Searcy Weed
Sara Buford Welch
Mary Beth Buchanan Weston
Allison Winter Wheeler
Kay Crosthwait Wheeler
Courtney White
Anne Whitfield
Margaret Ann Little Whitsett
Sara Landman Whitworth
Pam McElwee Wikle
Stephanie I. Wilkins
Cintra Eglin Willcox
Nancy Williams
Kathy Baird Wills
Alice Acuff Wilmer
Gloria Clark Wilson
Beth Machtolff Wise
Nancy Orgain Woltersdorf
Susan Hay Woodroof
Evelyn Barnett Wright
Lindsey McFarlan Wright
Jerry Ann Aycock Wynn
Talitha Bentley Yokley
Kelley Golden Zelickson

Index

Pine Seedlings near Greens

Chip Cooper

The Robert Trent Jones Golf Trail winds its way through Alabama offering golfers a variety of superb public courses each with its own distinctive character. The Scottish-style Highlands course at Hampton Cove is framed by a dramatic mountain backdrop.

Bibliography

Brown, Mary Ward. "Fruit of the Season." *Tongues of Flame.*
New York: E. P. Dutton/Seymour Lawrence, 1986.

Capote, Truman. *A Christmas Memory.* New York: Vintage
Books, a division of Random House, Inc., 1993.

Capote, Truman. *The Thanksgiving Visitor.* New York: Random
House, Inc., 1967.

Fitzgerald, Zelda. Excerpts from Zelda Fitzgerald: *The Collected
Writings,* edited by Matthew J. Bruccoli (Copyright© 1991
by The Trustees u/a dated 7/3/75 Created by Frances
Scott Fitzgerald Smith) used by permission of Scribner,
an imprint of Simon & Schuster, Inc.

Flagg, Fannie. *Fried Green Tomatoes at the Whistle Stop Cafe.*
New York: Random House, Inc., 1987.

Gilchrist, Ellen. *Net of Jewels.* Boston: Little, Brown and
Company Publishers, 1992.

Keller, Helen. *The Story of My Life.* Mahwah, New Jersey:
Watermill Press, 1980.

Lee, Harper. *To Kill A Mockingbird.* Philadelphia & New York:
J. B. Lippincott Company.

McCammon, Robert R. Reprinted with the permission of Simon
& Schuster Inc. from *Boy's Life* by Robert R. McCammon.
Copyright ©1991 by the McCammon Corporation.

Weeden, Maria Howard. "The Cotton Bloom." *Shadows on
the Wall.* Huntsville, Alabama: Burritt Museum, 1962.

Windham, Kathryn Tucker. *Alabama: One Big Front Porch.*
Huntsville, Alabama: Strode Publishers, Inc., 1975.

To order
Sweet Home Alabama
or **Huntsville Heritage**
Cookbooks, write or call:

The Junior League of Huntsville
Cookbook Publications
P.O. Box 816, Huntsville, Alabama 35804

Phone: (205) 883-9120   FAX: (205) 883-9162